Kathleen Farstad

TALES
of Successes with
KIDS

TALES
of Successes with
KIDS

From Parents and Educators
Who Use Love and Logic

The Love and Logic
PRESS Inc.

AMERICA'S PARENTING EXPERTS

The Love and Logic Press, Inc.

2207 Jackson Street, Golden, CO 80401-2300

800-338-4065 www.loveandlogic.com

Library of Congress Cataloging-in-Publication Data

Fay, Jim.

Tales of successes with kids : from parents and educators who use love and logic / Jim Fay.-- 1st ed.

p. cm.

Includes index.

ISBN 1-930429-40-1 (Paperback : alk. paper)

1. Parent and child--Anecdotes. 2. Child rearing--Anecdotes. 3. Teaching--Anecdotes. 4. Teachers--Anecdotes. 5. Discipline of children--Anecdotes. I. Title.

HQ755.85.F45 2003

306.874--dc21

2002156790

Project Coordinator: Carol Thomas
Editing by Jason Cook, Denver, CO
Cover design by Michael Snell, Shade of the Cottonwood, Topeka, KS
Interior design by Michael Snell, Shade of the Cottonwood, Topeka, KS

Contents

Tales of Successes with Kids

It was an accident. My becoming a storyteller, that is.

I needed to fill some instructional time in the first college class I was planning to teach. Why? It was because I believed that I didn't have enough subject matter. I needed a lot more material to fill the number of instructional hours required by the university.

In desperation I decided to reinforce each concept to be taught with an example out of my own experience. Translated, that means that I would fill up some time so that no one would realize that I didn't know enough to teach the class. What did I do? I used at least one story to reinforce each concept I planned to teach.

The first class was wildly successful. Evaluations were great. There were many references to how enjoyable the stories were. For some reason, I discounted all the comments about the value of the stories. All I could think about were my own inadequacies.

Sad to say, those were the days when I thought the more you taught, the better you were. Since then I've learned that less is more. Great teachers offer fewer concepts with a lot of reinforcement. And their students leave with more usable information and skills that are better developed.

I've also learned how the brain learns by connecting new ideas to those already mastered. So what do stories have to do with this? Stories cause the brain to do just that. As you hear a story, your brain associates what is happening in the story with what it already knows. You connect to the story thinking, "Yes, that's true. That's what it's like. I know that." Then as the storyteller adds a new or different twist to what's happening in the story, your brain makes a new connection and stores your new knowledge. Voilà, you have learned and will remember what you've learned.

Since learning about this I have devoted my life to learning how to tell stories. This is one of the reasons people tell me that they studied with me years ago and that they are still using what they learned. It also explains why people's lives are changed even when they have attended only one Love and Logic presentation. Love and Logic is taught with stories.

Another great result of my association with stories is that every day I meet people who have learned about Love and Logic. Guess what they want to talk about? You're right. They want to tell me stories about how they have used Love and Logic and how it has changed their lives.

Little by little, it occurred to me that all these stories should be shared with the world. Each and every one spreads the gifts of Love and Logic and provides hope and confidence for those wishing for a better quality of life.

We started collecting these stories, intent upon creating this book. It is best not to read the book all at once. Keep it where you can read one story each day. Remember that each person who has submitted a story to this book is a person whose life has been changed by Love and Logic. The same thing will happen to you as each story adds to, and reinforces all that wonderful learning that is already stored in your brain. Each time you tell one of these stories, you will be reinforcing your new knowledge, and your Love and Logic skills will be easier to remember and use.

And by the way, we are still collecting stories. We'd love to have yours to place in our next edition of *Tales of Successes with Kids*.

JIM FAY

Introduction

One of the greatest joys for us at the Love and Logic Institute is reading the many wonderful stories we receive from our supporters. It is truly inspiring to hear how Love and Logic has changed the lives of parents, educators, and kids.

We would like to thank all of those who have so kindly shared their successes. We would also like to share their stories with you. We hope you enjoy them as much as we have.

PART 1

Toddlers

*A*ren't they great—those wonderful little beings who come into our lives so sweet and innocent? They change our lives forever. And sometimes those changes can be a little overwhelming. They can start challenging us early in their lives. And so they should. That's how they learn. That's how they become independent. That's how they become wise. And isn't that what we all want?

But wait, do you have to let them control the entire household? The answer is a resounding "No!" Although life as you knew it, "prechild," has changed forever, it doesn't have to be for the worse. In fact, by using Love and Logic from a very early age, you can raise a wonderful child. One who will become a responsible, caring, and ethical adult...and meanwhile, not run you ragged.

Let's see how some parents established healthy control early and handled their little ones by using Love and Logic techniques.

After all the mistakes I made with my son, and after seeing how well the Love and Logic approach worked with him, I was determined that my daughter (two and a half years his junior) would have the full benefit of my newly acquired wisdom. Sure enough, age two comes around and Kelly starts to challenge me—whining, tantrums, the whole bit. But I was up to the challenge, and handling it was a piece of cake. No shoes in winter? No problem! No food you like? No problem! Now she's three and Love and Logic is the way she interacts with the world. Her older brother spilled his milk the other day. Kelly instantly says, "Bummer! What are you going to do about that, Philip?" My son says, "Clean it up I guess." Kelly continues, "Want to hear what other kids do?" My son says, "No, not really." My wife and I had to dip behind the kitchen counter to share a giggle. Parenting on autopilot is the way to go.

RICK RADDATZ

As suggested by Love and Logic, we have tried to give our three-year-old, Stuart, as many choices as possible during the day. This had been going really well for about a month, and Stuart seemed to be enjoying these choices and was easier to get along with. One day, we realized it really had sunk in. We were in the car on the way home from dinner, and Lucy, our fifteen-month-old, was crying in her car seat. Stuart picked up one of his toys and said, "Lucy, you have two choices. Either stop crying or don't have the toy."

It was amazing to see that he picked up on using the choices during a difficult time.

JULIE BRABBS

I'm an area manager for the Head Start preschool program. Several weeks ago I was in one of the classrooms I supervise. We do lunch "family style" with an adult at each table of children. We use disposable Styrofoam trays and utensils. I had three boys at my table that day, ages three to five years old. The children are taught and expected to clean up after themselves when they are finished—dump out any leftover milk, throw away their tray, utensils, napkin, and milk carton. Then they go to circle time. I'm not in the classroom on a regular basis like the classroom staff is, so I'm not as familiar with all the children and how cooperative or uncooperative they are. On this day, the teacher was over on the carpet where circle time occurs, talking to the children who had arrived and encouraging the other children to finish, clean up, and come join them. She informed them that "Louie" would be visiting them today—a puppet that she uses periodically that they all enjoy. Two of my young lads were looking her way and starting in that direction without taking care of their things. So I walked over to one, bent down to his level with my hand gently on his shoulder, and quietly said, "You're welcome to go to circle time when you've taken care of your things." He looked at the inviting circle, looked at his stuff on the table, processed for about thirty seconds, then disposed of his stuff and went to circle time! I was impressed! I repeated the process and got a similar response from the second lad. Wow! No problem for either of us!

"You're welcome to [do this] when you [do that]" has become one of my favorite lines. It takes some practice to apply it at opportune times, but the more I use it, the easier it gets.

KAREN KUBIAK

I attended one of the Love and Logic seminars recently and it has changed my life. I am a professional nanny as well as a mother of a three-year-old. My son comes to work with me, so I provide care for three toddlers all together (the others are three and two years old). After attending the conference, I decided to put the Love and Logic technique to the test. My employers have a trampoline for the kids, which has a safety net. Great fun right? Not for me. I dreaded every moment they were on that thing. It was a constant battle trying to keep everyone happy. I heard screams of, "Angela, he's pushing me!" "Stop bouncing right next to me!" "Stop it!" "Angela, she jumped on me on purpose!" And the crying—constant crying even though nobody was really hurt. I was constantly saying, "Christian, don't push," "Jordan, you're hurting her," "If you can't play nice, then you're not going to get gummies later." And so on and so forth. This battle went on until they finally got sick of jumping or I bribed them to do something else.

After the conference, I tried this method: "Okay guys, let's go on the trampoline, but I only let kids who don't scream or fight stay on." Well, after about five seconds they were all fighting. "Uh-oh. Looks like it's time we do something else." And I removed them from the trampoline instantly amid pleas of, "We're sorry, Angela," "But we won't fight anymore, Angela." I just smiled and said, "I know." Then I got the "I'm not going to be your friend anymore!" I just smiled and said, "Bummer!"

Now this was quite a shock for these kids, whom I'd raised since birth and who had me trained to give them warning after warning, bribe after bribe. It took about one minute for them to find something else to play with. About twenty minutes later they wanted to go on the trampoline. I smiled and said, "Sure, but I only let kids who don't fight or scream stay on." It was the same thing again. Even though the kids weren't catching on right away, a lot of pressure was taken off me—trying to get them to be quiet, trying to make them not scream, trying to keep them playing nicely. All I had to do was say "Uh-oh" and take them off the trampoline.

Ten minutes later they asked again and I smiled and said, "Sure." Well, let me tell you, Christian looked right up at me and said, "We won't fight and we won't scream, okay Angela?" Then he looked at the other two and said, "Okay guys, no fighting." And they didn't.

That "training session" took about forty minutes total and I haven't had a day of grief on the trampoline since. After two years of dreading it, now it finally is an opportunity for us to have a good time.

ANGELA RHEINGANS

This is so great, I just had to share it with you. I have a two-year-old in my class this year. I am always heard saying, "Ooooh I don't think I'd dooo thaaaat." The other day during rest time I heard a cute little voice say to some other child, "Ooooh tink I do dat."

ANNA MARIE ELLIS

I was sitting in the big rocking chair in our family room watching my two grandchildren, Christopher (three) and Marissa (eighteen months), playing with their barn and farmyard toy animals. My mind reflected back to six weeks earlier when their mother (our daughter-in-law) had died suddenly as the result of a terrible postoperative infection. She had gone into the hospital a few days before Christmas for what should have been an overnight stay, but she never came home again. My heart ached almost continually for my grandchildren, wondering how their little minds could make sense of the sudden loss of their mother.

I had been watching the children all morning while our son went to a business meeting. I was recovering from hip surgery, but my husband was working out of our home office that day, so I knew I had backup if I needed it. The children had been playing quite peacefully for nearly half an hour when I began hearing some arguing. Christopher had been playing with the little pig that goes with the barnyard set and his little sister reached over and took it. "No, no Rissa!" I heard him say. "No, no! My pig." She held it closer to her. "I said, my pig Rissa! Gimme my pig." She pulled it further away from him. I was just recovering from hip surgery, and it took me a moment to get out of my chair. I heard his one final battle cry before he took action. "Rissa, gimme my *pig!*" Then in an instant he clenched his teeth on her forearm. The pig, of course, was immediately released from her grasp, but his teeth marks were embedded in her arm. She ran to me shrieking and sobbing.

I sat back down in my chair and comforted her for a few minutes. Christopher was sitting across the room looking confused and guilty. When Marissa settled down and was calm, I called Christopher over to me, and he immediately started to cry. I put my arm around him and he sobbed, saying, "Gramgra (his name for me)—she took my pig! I told her, 'No, no Rissa,' but she took my pig. She took my pig!"

"I know she took your pig Christopher," I said. "And I know you wanted it back. But do we bite people to get our toys back?" He looked at me. "No." "That's right, Christopher. We don't bite to get our toys back. If Rissa takes something you are playing with and you need help, what could you do instead of biting her?" He shrugged his shoulders. His vocabulary skills were quite limited despite the fact that he had just turned three. So I said, "If you need help, you can ask a grown-up. You can always ask grandma for help. But we do not bite people. We bite

5

apples, we bite food, but we do not bite people." He stood there, quietly crying, looking at me.

Before our daughter-in-law's death, she and our son had worked very hard on training the children using principles of Love and Logic. I knew she would have had him sit in time-out long enough to break the emotional spell and calm him down, so I went into the kitchen, got a kitchen chair, and brought it back into the family room. (I had other options, such as putting him in his room for a little time-out, but every instinct in me told me to keep him close. I did not want him in any way to feel abandoned.) I put the kitchen chair quite close to the chair I had been sitting in, picked him up and set him gently on it, and said, "Christopher, I'm going to set the timer for five minutes and when the buzzer rings, you can get down." He sat there for about one second, then slid off the chair and did a face-plant on the floor. He was really angry now. I picked him up and he started screaming and struggling.

I once heard Dr. Foster Cline say that the reason God made toddlers so little is so you can pick them up and change their location. So I picked him up and held him on my lap in the rocking chair until he calmed down. When he was calm, I stood up and gently set him onto the time-out chair again and repeated my instructions: "I will set the timer for five minutes. When the buzzer rings you can get down." I hadn't even sat down in my chair before he had thrown himself onto the floor again.

I was exhausted. I'd had total hip replacement only four weeks earlier and I didn't have a surplus of physical or emotional energy. But the aching in my hip wasn't my biggest problem. It was the aching in my tender grandmother's heart. This was a little boy whose mother had just died. I wondered what confusion, anger, and probably rage must be coursing through him, and with his limited vocabulary he couldn't even express it. Now for the second time, he lay on the floor screaming.

There was a little voice deep inside me that was saying, "Just let him go. He knows what he did was wrong. He's been through enough. So he didn't sit and stay in the time-out chair—so what? Do it another day. He's tired, maybe he's hungry, and he did tell her to give the pig back."

But there was another voice inside of me: a louder and surer and stronger voice that said, "This child's life is spinning out of control. He has lost the security of his mother, and he can't even comprehend where she is. His world must feel like the most unsure, unstable place." After years of teaching Love and Logic, I was well acquainted with the concept of the Control V (the V of love). He may have felt like he was in a freefall, but I knew where he needed to land: in the security of loving and logical limits. I was filled with a peace and resolve that the most important thing I could do for my grandson that day was to not let him down. I would not let him crash through the security of loving and logical limits. He needed that security more now than he ever had in his life.

So *I* sat down in the time-out chair, picked him up, and held him on my lap. He was crying and struggling and sobbing, "But Gramgra, Rissa took my pig—she took my pig." I gently wrapped my arms around him, held him close, put his face close to mine, and began rocking him back and forth in the chair. To his sobs about the injustice of his pig being taken, I quietly said, "I know. I know. She took your pig and that made you so mad." Eventually after about six or eight minutes his sobs had all but subsided. Occasionally between sniffles he would say, "But she took my pig, Gramgra." And I would reply, "I know sweetheart, I know."

After about ten minutes he was completely calm. The problem was, he had not yet stayed on the time-out chair. He had only been *practicing* how you do it with Grandma. So I stood up, put him back on the chair, and repeated my original instructions: "As soon as the timer rings, you can get down." I absolutely could not believe it when he slid off the chair and started crying again.

I was so exhausted that *I* wanted to cry. But there was no stopping now. I picked him up, sat down on the time-out chair with him on my lap, and we started all over again. He cried, I gave him love and empathy, we rocked gently back and forth, he settled down, and occasionally reminded me in the midst of his crying, "I told her 'No, no' Gramgra." After another ten minutes he was calm again. I stood up, put him on the chair, and he stayed! No crying, no sobbing, no protesting—he stayed! When the buzzer rang, he looked and me and asked sweetly, "I get down now, Gramgra?" I said yes. I held him close and asked him what he thought he could do that would make his sister feel better. He said, "I give her a hug? I say, 'Sorry Rissa'?"

So off he went with apologies and hugs and Toddler Training Session 101 was over for the morning. Exhausting? Yes! Worth every minute? Without question! Why? Because he learned at a very tender age a few important lessons about his grandmother: that I say what I mean and mean what I say, and that he can count on me to provide loving and logical limits.

CHRIS HALL

I came home yesterday to find that things had visibly not gone well with my two girls (ages four and six), who had been with a somewhat new baby-sitter for three hours (my girls are on a bickering and rivalry "rampage" that will unsettle almost anyone!). They were both whining and crying at full tilt, the young and inexperienced baby-sitter was clearly shell-shocked, and the entire scenario was out of control.

After things settled down and the baby-sitter recounted her difficulties with my two little sweetums, I asked them what they planned to do about the problem. "What problem?" was their response—the problem for them being that they might have scared away a really nice baby-sitter (and might have to get a mean and awful one since a nice one won't want to come if they are going to act that way).

They're young and they struggled a bit with some solutions, so I tried the textbook Love and Logic question, "Would you like to know what other kids have done in this situation?" Which worked like a charm! First time it's ever worked quite so well, probably because I let them struggle with it for a while. I threw out the proverbial most awful solution, which they nixed right away (of course!), and then we moved on to some more likely ones.

They decided that it costs less per hour to hire a nice baby-sitter to come stay with you when you're being cooperative and agreeable, and more per hour to hire someone to come care for you when your behavior is really awful and you and your sister are bickering and fighting, since it takes so much more energy on the baby-sitter's part. They agreed (tearfully) to share the difference in the hourly rate for those three hours. They also decided to apologize and tell the baby-sitter they hoped she'd return someday, and because it only cost 10¢ for a phone call, versus 34¢ to mail a letter, they dialed her up and issued a very sincere and heartfelt apology (also with a few tears!). If you could have seen the sincere and huge crocodile tears out of the little one's eyes as she opened the jar where she is saving her allowance to buy an American Girl doll—it was as sad and pitiful as I've ever seen her. She was just horrified that her doll savings was going toward something else.

I can't thank you enough. I think this lesson is likely to stick for a while. It was an SLO (significant learning opportunity) for all of us! It worked so well, and I got to remain calm, cool, empathetic, and sane while the consequences I gave issued the lesson. No need to scold or raise my voice or punish or even issue an empty apology to the baby-sitter. I think it all really sunk in with the little ones.

You're the best, Jim Fay! Undoubtedly many more SLOs to go before this rivalry gets manageable, but I'm on the right track to help them through it in a productive way!

THANKS AGAIN!
MAUREEN M. KNAPP

I just wanted to drop you folks a note and tell you how great your concepts are. We are the parents of twin five-year-olds and have used the Love and Logic principles for two years now. We are now on our fourth copy of *Parenting with Love and Logic* and we have purchased three copies of *Love and Logic Magic for Early Childhood*. Every time we start discussing children's behavior with our friends and neighbors, they end up "borrowing" our copy and we never see it again.

The amazing thing is how well the concepts work and how much better you feel as a parent after using them. Before discovering Dr. Foster Cline and Jim Fay in an airport one night, I was at my wits' end trying to "control" my two-year-olds. Now we are a team and they are responsible for their actions. It's such a relief not to be the Drill Sergeant anymore.

I am sure that you get hundreds of letters like this one all the time, but please pass on thanks from my wife and myself. It has made a world of difference in our life and that of our children.

MIKE RAPPORT

When our oldest, Brett, was about three, we took our first big trip to Disney World. The heat and the hurrying about can take its toll on everyone, and Brett's behavior was taking a turn for the worse. We were standing in the *long* line for the "Flying Dumbo" ride, and his standing-in-line skills were pretty well shot. He was whining, tugging on my arm, getting mouthy, etc. I told him that he was being rude to the other people in the line—they didn't like his whining, and he kept bumping into others as he jerked around. I hadn't actually taken any Love and Logic courses yet, so I must admit that I gave him a warning or two. I told him that if he didn't stop, we'd have to leave the line because he was being so disruptive to others. Of course, he couldn't do any better, so we left the line. I heard a couple of stunned parents make comments about the fact that it was about time a parent actually *did* something, rather than just threaten.

I took Brett to the closest refreshment stand, under a nice shady tree. We had a cold drink while we waited for the rest of our group to finish the ride. We then rejoined our party for what was left of the day. I'm convinced that Brett was truly exhausted and overwhelmed by the heat and hectic pace, and the relaxing cold drink was just what he needed. But of course he also learned that I really meant it when I told him what the consequences would be for poor behavior.

For the rest of the trip, all I had to do was mention the "Flying Dumbos" and he immediately shaped up! The magic actually lasted for several years—all it took was a reminder and he behaved.

Brett is a big boy now—fourteen to be exact! Like a lot of teens, he's pretty slow in the bathroom, and especially so on Sunday mornings when we're trying to get to church on time. Finally one Sunday, when it was clear that we were going to be late, I hollered into his room, "I'll be leaving at 9:15. I hope you make it." (Yes, by now, I had taken Love and Logic courses.) Needless to say, he didn't make it.

Next Sunday, same story. Unfortunately, I was wondering if this idea was backfiring—maybe he was just trying to get out of going to church! (Although it would seem really stupid to spend all that time getting ready and then not make it at all.)

On the third Sunday, I wondered what would happen. As it was getting close to departure time, he called to me, "Mom, please don't leave without me, I'll be ready in time—I really want to go to church this week." And he was ready on time. Wow! It worked!

BEV BLAMER

I had the pleasure of attending Jim Fay's conference in Highland Park, Texas, and wanted to share a success story with you. I've been retraining myself using Love and Logic techniques and they have really changed things in my family. Here's my story:

My five-year-old son has been throwing temper tantrums since he was tiny. Believe me, he has this down to an art. He would run after me, grab my ankles, and continue his tantrum before I could wrestle him into his room. I did what all of the other books said—I would just ignore him and walk away. This did not work, the tantrums continued.

Several weeks ago, after I had listened to one of the Love and Logic tapes, he started to throw a tantrum. I said, "Uh-oh, some bedroom time is coming up." I took him to his room and told him to stomp harder, add his fists, and cry louder. And I said it all with a smile on my face. He thought I had lost my marbles: but he has not thrown a tantrum in almost four weeks.

Thank you for giving me this practical and easy solution that actually works.

CINDY STANLEY

My four-year-old entered the prekindergarten (K–4) program in our public school system. This was the first year for the program and the first year of real school for my child.

I know my child and I anticipated that I would be getting a call before long about his behavior. My daycare provider also knew it. We had discussed before how each time she hires a new "teacher" he watches for the adult's weaknesses and tries to force his way into being the boss of the classroom. I reviewed my Love and Logic material and listened to my tapes. I was ready.

The complaint came the second week into the school year. My child was refusing to do what the rest of the class was doing. He tried to get the teacher involved in fights by using the phrases, "No, I don't want to" and "I don't have to." She said that he was a bright child, and that she hated to complain, but he was causing a problem in the class because some of the other children were beginning to follow his lead. It was a Friday.

Our conversation (my son and I) on the way home went something like this:

ME: It's sad that you are not getting along with your teacher.
        It's really a problem. What are you going to do about it?

SON: I don't know.

ME: Would you like to know what some kids have done?
        (My heart was beating wildly.)

SON: Okay.

ME: Some kids keep on yelling at the teachers and roll around
        on the floor and create so much trouble that the other
        kids can't do their schoolwork.

SON: Well, what happens to them?

ME: They are asked to leave the class and they don't get to go
        to kindergarten the next year.

SON: And they don't learn to read?

ME: Not for a long time. But some kids decide it's more fun to
        be helpers and help the teachers do the lessons in class.

SON: What if they don't want to color?

ME: Well, some kids do it anyway because they know they'll
        get to do something else a little later. (My son was silent,

so I asked again:) Do you have any ideas about what you
can do to solve your problem?

SON: No, and I don't want to talk about it anymore.

It was so difficult not to talk about it anymore. It was difficult not to resort
back to what my parents would have said. It was even more difficult on
Monday when I let him off at daycare and said only, "I hope you can solve
your problem with your teacher, but I'll love you even if you don't get to
go to kindergarten next year. Let me know how it works out."

The next week the teacher asked if she could talk to me in private for a
minute. My child was on the playground and saw us talking. The teacher
asked, "What have you done to your son? He has made a complete turnaround. I have never seen a child's behavior change so rapidly. I thought
he was going to be a problem all year."

I explained that it was Love and Logic. I recounted what I did. I told her I
was just a novice and not sure I was doing it right, but I was planning to
attend a Jim Fay lecture the next month for some more tips. I agreed to
give her the information on the lecture and a catalog.

I got in the car and my son wanted to know what was going on. "Your
teacher was just telling me how proud she was of you in class." "I know,"
my son smiled. "I was the helper today. You know what, Mom? It's really
fun to be the helper. I'm going to try to be the helper again."

Thanks to the people at Love and Logic for sharing your child-rearing
knowledge. You are making a difference one parent and child at a time.

CATHY MCFARLAND

God has given me many wonderful things in my life! Bringing Love and
Logic into it is just one of them. I must start first with how I was raised.
My mother and father divorced when I was three and my mother (who
spoke very little English at the time) was left to raise three daughters on
her own—basically. My mother worked very hard to give us a good life.
But all the work left her tired and stressed out.

Whenever we would act up, her solution was to scare us into never misbehaving again. She would rant and rave, slap us anywhere she could reach us, and then refuse to speak to us for a few days or a week—until we felt so guilty that we would be forced to apologize for basically being kids trying to grow up. There were no consequences for our actions other than the lack of love from our mother. I'm sure I don't need to go any further here, because we all know (those of us who practice Love and Logic) what the pattern was after that.

Now onto the middle part of the success story. I am all grown up (yeah, right!) and I have a daughter of my own. She is three, and a handful. She begins to assert her individuality and I am taken by complete surprise. What do you think I do when she acts up? I rant and rave. I don't slap because I refuse to hit my children, but I take my love away from her and make her feel guilty for what she has done. And not until she is in tears and saying what a bad child she is do I give her a hug. Of course, then I feel guilty and we go buy a toy.

On to the best part of the story. I am a childcare provider and I am attending my first conference put on by the organization for childcare providers that I have joined. I take a class called "Love and Logic." With this class, my world changes. I learn the most important thing—that I don't have to take the love away in order to teach my child to make good choices. I learn about giving choices, such as, "Do you want to wear your shoes or carry them?" This has been one of the most wonderful sayings I have learned. I also learned the "Uh-oh, how sad" phrase and much much more.

Presently I am a mother of two. I have been doing childcare for five years. I have spread the word of Love and Logic like wildfire. I have shared many techniques with my daycare clients, and I am continuing to learn and grow as a parent, a professional, and a human being. My son has grown up with Love and Logic and is pretty well adjusted. My daughter, the three-year-old in this story, has some anger issues (I wonder why?), but with my demonstrations of taking care of myself, and respecting her by holding her accountable (and lots of hugs no matter what the issue) she and we will work through this.

One of the best things I like about Love and Logic is that it is doable. It is not something that only doctors or counselors can understand or implement. Any parent (no matter what their age) and any professional can start using it today—right now! Also, one can grow with Love and Logic: the more you practice it the better you get. And before you know it, you are doing it so naturally that your kids are doing it with their friends. The hardest thing about Love and Logic is that not all adults use it. And if you have a Love and Logic child, they can get confused when the other adults in their life (teachers, leaders, etc.) don't show them the same respect and accountability, or even the flexibility, that they are shown at home. We need to teach—reach more parents and teachers with these techniques.

Thank you for Love and Logic. You saved my relationship with my children and you saved me from feeling guilty and powerless when dealing with my own children or the kids I provide childcare for. I can now say that I am raising responsible and caring children!

HEIDI M. HOLDEN

I attended my first Love and Logic parenting class when my only son, Grant, was five months old. Being a forty-year-old first-time parent, I was hungry for any and all information I could get. I came home from the first session excited and confident that parenting isn't as hard as everyone has led me to believe.

Your information and advice are wonderful! I have now taken the class four times and I'm enrolled to take it again in a few months. Repetitive education in your program enables me, most of the time, to react appropriately because it's known.

Really, the only challenging and embarrassing situation happened when Grant was twenty-two months old. We went to the mall only to pick up a few books at the bookstore. The line and wait were a bit long and he was somewhat restless. However, he picked up a couple of books on a table and contently looked through them as I made the purchase. I told him we were leaving and to put the books away. Clenching a paperback in each hand, he loudly and firmly says, "No!" After asking again and getting the same reaction, I quickly grab a book from one of his hands and put it down. In a split second he throws himself, chest down, on the floor, screaming and crying while holding on to the other book for dear life.

I was in shock, as he had never had a tantrum before. And of course the store is packed with onlookers, so embarrassment sets in.

What do I do as I'm looking at his backside? What would Jim Fay or Foster Cline do? My mind is racing through the six-week Love and Logic course in seconds. People are looking at me. People are looking at Grant. People are trying hard not to look at either of us. Then, ah ha, it hits me. Do nothing. Wait. Who cares what these people might think? Take care of the adult first. Then a couple walks by and the man says very nicely, "Been there, done that." The weight lifted off my shoulders and what seemed like ten minutes was actually about one. Grant stopped, placed the book on the table, held my hand, and smiled. Out we walked. I felt every eye on my back as we walked away. I felt their minds thinking, "Well, she handled that with coolness."

Thank you Love and Logic! My natural behavior would have been to grab him, kicking and screaming, as fast as possible and get out. Then lecture him all the way home. I didn't even bring up the subject in the car and it's not happened again.

As a salesperson, it's natural for me to give two choices. However, I'm much more conscious of this because of Love and Logic. Our son just turned three a few months ago. About this same time, we were driving and I must have given him two options for something. His response was, "You take a choice, Mom!" But I have not used the word "choice." Here I am driving and trying to write a mental note to tell this to my Love and Logic instructor, John Roope. At first I thought that Grant has my parenting classes figured out. But I realized he always says this when he doesn't care which option.

JANELL B. FARMER

I am a mother of three young children, ages five, three, and one. Last October I was given the opportunity to attend the training in Colorado to become a facilitator. I had never heard of Love and Logic before and I didn't know any of the techniques they taught. I spent four days in the training and I left a changed woman! I especially loved the "Energy Drain" and the

"Uh-Oh Song." I came home and immediately began using them. My daughter reacted amazingly with the "Uh-Oh Song," while my son showed the greatest improvement with the "Energy Drain."

About a week after I had returned home, things were going okay, but my kids had started to fight the boundaries a bit. I thought I had messed up and was getting frustrated, until one night when my three-year-old son was following me around like a puppy and I snapped at him to get in his room. I went in my room and cried because I had messed up again!

A short time later, I went to his room to check on him, and he proved to me that I had been doing something right. He looked up at me and said, "Mommy, when you yell at me it really drains my energy. Would you like to know how some mommies give their kids energy back? Some mommies throw the TV at their kids—would that give me my energy back?" I promptly smiled and said, "No sweetie, that probably wouldn't give you your energy back." "Some mommies say they're sorry. Would that give me my energy back?" "Yes honey, that would probably help." So I gave him the biggest hug I could and he came back with, "That was pretty good, but I still don't have all my energy back, would you like to know what would give me more energy back?" "Of course I would, sweetie." "Some mommies say they love their little boy and then help them clean up their room. Would that give me more energy back?" "That would probably work very well." I then told him that I loved him very much and we cleaned up his room together.

Now, some might say that he was manipulating me, but the way I saw it was that I must have been doing something right after only a week, to have him using the technique so well.

Love and Logic has been a life-altering experience. Before I went to the training, I would spank my kids and yell at them, not because I wanted to, but because I didn't know what else to do. Now I'm able to teach other people this amazing program and help them experience the same great change that I have. Thank you Love and Logic!

MINDY GRAHAM

I was taking my three-year-old son through the drive-thru at "Burger Chef" and while we were in line, I gave him the choice between a hamburger or chicken. He said, "I'd like chicken, Dad!" As our meal was being handed to us, he started whining, "No wait, I want a hamburger! I want a hamburger!" I had only just finished the Love and Logic book, but I hadn't had a chance to use any of the techniques yet and was a little unsure of what to say. I wanted to say, "Stop whining!" or "Be happy that you have food." But instead, I kept silent while his whining got worse. Then my newfound knowledge kicked in. I said, "I understand just how you feel Philip. Back when I was your age, sometimes I would order the wrong thing, and then I wouldn't get what I wanted." He stopped, and got this weird, twisted expression on his face. It was obvious he was thinking, and I tried to keep from laughing. Then he said, "Well, when I was your age, I'd back up and get you what you wanted!" I couldn't hold it in, and I started laughing, and he laughed too. Then he said, "Next time I'm going to order a hamburger."

RICK RADDATZ

We adopted a special needs baby after we adopted a family of four kids (more chances to apply Love and Logic were in store for us). Angela has spina bifida, hydrocephalus, and cerebral palsy, which is a nasty mix for any child. We are really acquainted with the medical community.

Ang gave a real opportunity one day to practice "choices." She had a grueling session of physical therapy with Jil, whom she liked, and exercises, which she didn't. Just keeping her head up was real work for our four-year-old and anything else was extra hard work. On the way home from the hospital my wife needed to stop at Wal-Mart. Ang decided that that was just too much and let us know it with "dry-eyed wailing." She likes to control what she can and figured that included us. Oh boy, another Love and Logic moment.

I had read that giving choices will give a child power in a situation and that the outcome can be directed by the parent without a war of the wills happening. Angela is one strong-willed little girl and was going to perfect her skills on us, she probably thought.

We had parked the car and I asked Ang, "Would you like to shop with me or with Mother?" That elicited a wailing explosion. I said to Ruth, "I guess that Ang would like to stay in the car with me. Have fun shopping." Ruth really does like to shop, I don't. She left and I got to stay in the car with the now screaming child. One can take that only so long (don't think kids don't know that), so I calmly said, "Since it's such a nice spring day, I will wait outside the car. Let me know when you are ready to shop." More screaming and some calculating looks. I waited just outside of her range of vision. I observed her looking for me. When the wailing would decrease I would repeat, "Are you ready to shop yet?" Wailing explosion once again. "Just let me know when you are ready."

Some women were looking at me now. I just smiled at them and said I'm doing a Love and Logic training session. They left in a hurry. I thought they might call social services about this and I could share a wonderful resource with them.

Anyway, I was timing this episode and it had already lasted six minutes. She decreased the wailing and I tried it again with the same results. Finally, at eight minutes and forty-five seconds the wailing stopped completely. I asked the same question and she said yes.

I brought a cart and, ah ha, more choices. "Would you like to ride in the seat or the cart?" She chose the inside of the cart. When we got into the store I thought that another choice could be made. Choices are actually fun. "Would you like to shop with Mother or with me?" She chose Mother because she knows Mother buys more and her chances of getting more are multiplied. I am rather focused and buy what I need and then get out of there.

The rest of the experience was actually pleasant and our very exhausted little girl (trying to get one's own way is tiring) really liked the choices she had made. We made our twenty-five-mile trip home in a relaxed manner. Once again, thanks for Love and Logic.

ROBERT AND RUTH RIDDELL

My daughter, Lizzy, is four months old and hasn't reached a challenging stage yet (I'm sure there are many who say even this age is a challenge!). I was fortunate to be able to attend a Love and Logic seminar while I was pregnant, and am using this time to practice what I've learned. When

Lizzy's older, I hope to be well seasoned. For now, I am very conscious of how I speak to her.

For example, one day while at the doctor's office, I stopped in to speak to a nurse who had helped me throughout my pregnancy. Lizzy started getting fussy and I realized how tired she was. I placed her in her seat while saying, "Okay, I'm going to put you in your seat and you're going to go to sleep" (an unenforceable statement). I realized this and said, "No, I can't make you go to sleep, I'm going to put you in your seat and create a sleeping environment for you. It's up to you to sleep." The nurse burst out with a fit of laughter. I asked her if it weren't true what I had just said; I can't force her to sleep, but I can make her comfortable enough to woo her to Lala Land. "Yes," replied the nurse, who added that she wished other parents would talk to their children that way.

Another time I was with a home visitor and Lizzy began to fuss. "Oh, are you hungry? Here we go…" I looked at Lizzy eye to eye (the only way I can get her attention) and said, "Lizzy, do you hear how calmly I'm talking to you? I'm listening, you can talk to me." I realize this is a long stretch, telling a four-month-old to talk to me, but, and I'm very honest when I say this, she stopped crying and babbled—angrily, but she babbled! I replied, "I understand you're upset, but I like it when you talk to me." My visitor, who is very used to how I talk to my daughter, was surprised that Lizzy stopped crying and actually tried to talk to me. I used that opportunity to talk about Love and Logic.

I'm very glad I had the opportunity to attend a Love and Logic seminar while I was pregnant. I still fall back on my old ways, but I can fine-tune while Lizzy is a baby, and not have to try to change later when I have problems. I can already tell I'll be using these techniques a lot on my child.

TAMIEKA DUNKLIN

My neighbor told me this story and I wanted to share it with you. Her oldest child is three and is really getting the hang of the Love and Logic principles. Last week his mom got pulled over for running a red light. After the policeman left, the child said from the back seat, "Mommy, did you make a bad decision?" I think he's gotten the point!

SHANNON SECKINGER

Today was my designated day to put my "winter village" back into storage until next year. As I started boxing it up, William, my two-year-old, was curious of all those little pieces. He wanted to play with the little people but started throwing them around and kept doing so even after I told him no and helped him put them back. Inevitably, he got some "Uh-oh" time in his room. I let him out after a short time and noticed that he didn't go near the boxes again. A little while later he climbed up in my lap and looked at the boxes and pointed, saying, "Doan! Doan! Doan!" (that's toddler talk for "don't," just in case you need a translator).

Once again the "Uh-Oh Song" works for William. Score! I'm thinking, another triumph for Love and Logic. But I just hugged him and nodded seriously, "Yes, that's right, sweet pea!"

TAMARA VAN HOOSER

I had this couple in my class who began using "I love you too much to argue" with their six-year-old son. One day, when they were arguing with each other, their son ran up to them, grabbed each of them by the sleeve, and said, "Mommy, Daddy, remember, you love each other too much to argue." They immediately stopped, looked at their son, and hugged him and each other.

STEPHANIE BRYAN

My three-year-old daughter was the princess of dawdling. It was constantly a problem getting her to come to dinner, get out of the tub, put her coat on, etc. She was always too busy. The key for her was to give her choices. I began asking her, "Do you want to play for five more minutes or ten more minutes?" Both answers worked for me and she was left in control. It was a win/win situation.

RIA COLE

My daycare provider heard that Jim Fay was going to be in town and recommended going, as she had enjoyed hearing him speak years earlier. After hearing Jim speak I immediately ordered a starter package, realizing that Love and Logic was the commonsense answer I had been looking for.

My five-year-old daughter learned to tie her shoes at least a year ago, but always wants me to do it for her. I usually give in or suffer through crying and threats just trying to get the morning moving along a little faster. One Sunday morning we were getting ready to go out and she again asked me to tie her shoes. She was shocked when I told her she would need to pay me for my services. The "price" would be a particular baby doll, along with an extra set of clothes, a baby blanket, and a baby pillow.

While my daughter was thinking about this sacrifice, my husband was trying to find the car keys so that he could go golfing. I asked him if he needed help and he responded, "No, you'll probably make me pay with golf balls." He had not been able to go to Mr. Fay's seminar or listen to the tapes I had ordered, so he added, "You're not going to use that stuff on me!" Meanwhile, he found the keys by himself and I completed the task I was working on without interruption.

After attempting to talk me into another toy and some whining, she started to ask me what I would do with the baby doll and if I would be keeping it forever. "Yes," I said, "she will be mine to play with." My daughter finally brought me the baby doll I wanted along with my other requested items. I wrapped my new baby doll up in its blanket and then reached over to tie my daughter's shoes, but she pushed my hand away. I innocently told her that she had paid me and I would tie her shoes now. "No," she said, "I'll tie my own shoes so I can keep my baby doll."

A few days later she asked me what she had to give me to tie her shoes again. This really caught me off guard. I decided I had better up the "price" and said I would tie them in exchange for Maggie Karen, her favorite baby doll. I really think she was testing me to see if I had the guts to do this. I did. I tied her shoes and she went on her way without Maggie Karen. There was no fight, no threats, and no crying. It's been over a week without Maggie Karen and I have yet to tie another shoe. Now my daughter is trying to think up ways she can earn her baby doll back!

REBECCA DOWN

P.S. My husband has since started to listen to the Love and Logic tapes and is now using "that stuff" on me.

PART 2

Elementary Kids

s our children grow older, the challenges change. They're exposed to many new influences. They need to know how to problem-solve and be good decisionmakers on their own.

In the following pages you'll see how some great Love and Logic parents helped their children learn to make good decisions about school, friends, pets, chores, and everything in between, and to be responsible for their actions. These parents made their children do the majority of the thinking—while the parents learned to take good care of themselves. A great foundation for what is to come—the teen years.

Read, laugh, and learn—you'll find some wonderful stories full of love and encouragement.

What a difference your program has made with my Caitlin! A year ago, she was being bullied at school by another third-grader. One day after school, Caitlin told me that this bully had cornered her in the bathroom and began teasing her until she felt like crying and that she wanted some ideas on what to do.

As she was telling me the story, I forgot all my Love and Logic techniques and began ranting and raving and telling my daughter that I had had enough and that I was going to that school and things were going to change. I told Caitlin things like, "You go tell that little girl that if she doesn't leave you alone that your mother is going to come up to that school and take care of this problem and that your mother is going to call her mother." Well, my husband came in and suggested that I calm down and think things through; and yet I continued to rant and rave while Caitlin had this puzzled look on her face.

The next morning, I called my Love and Logic partner, Karen Harris, and explained what I had done and she suggested that I use the "guiding children to solve their own problems" technique instead. I agreed that I had mishandled the situation.

I anxiously waited for school to be out so that I could talk to Caitlin. Her first words to me were, "Mom, I don't need your help anymore. I went ahead and took care of it." My heart sank. I was almost afraid to ask her what she had done. I explained to her that I was wrong in what I said the night before and that I gave her some really bad ideas and that even grown-ups make mistakes. Well, before I could get through my explanation, Caitlin interrupted me by saying, "Oh, Mom, I didn't do anything you suggested. I didn't like any of those ideas. This morning I asked my teacher if I could go see the school counselor and when I went I asked for peer mediation. All three of us sat round in the counselor's office and talked until everything was all worked out." My mouth dropped open. Caitlin's parting comment to me as she was going to her room was, "You know what, Mom? I have a plan now and I know what to do if something happens again." As I stood there with tears in my eyes, my husband came up behind me and whispered, "I'm glad she didn't take your advice." Me too!

Caitlin is now nine and in the fourth grade. She is taking Tae Kwon Do. Last night as we were leaving class, Caitlin turned to me and said, "Well, you need to write that Love and Logic guy and tell him that Love and Logic is for kids too!" I asked her what she meant and she said that a kid in the class was making fun of her and telling her that she wasn't doing the kicks right and that she was moving too slowly. Caitlin said, "Mom, you know what I did? I smiled really nice at her and said very calmly, 'Thank you for sharing.' She kept trying to bother me and I just kept saying over and over, 'Thank you for sharing.'" And then Caitlin told me, "Mom, I know why you use that stuff; it really keeps you calm and I like that. It made me feel good." I said, "I thought you didn't like Love and Logic." She smiled and said, "I don't like it when you use it on me, but I love using it on others!" I gave my daughter a great big hug.

You know what the best part is? My daughter told me this story with such confidence. I could tell that she was extremely happy that she solved this "bullying" problem on her own. This is what your program is all about: kids feeling confident, feeling empowered, feeling responsible and accountable and in charge of their actions.

May this program continue to blossom all across the world—wherever there are children!

KELLY SMITH

Dear Love and Logic,

I thoroughly enjoy reading about the experiences of others and truly benefit from them. I wanted to share some exciting things that are happening with Love and Logic at our school. This is the second year that I have taught Parenting with Love and Logic through our school district. This school year many of our classrooms have adopted the Love and Logic approach to teaching children responsibility. This collaborative approach of having home and school on the same sheet of music has proven beneficial more often than not. Love and Logic has helped many of our educators slow down and handle situations in a calmer manner. It is fun to watch them grow into empathic, loving, stress-reduced individuals.

One seven-year-old boy who has benefited from the Love and Logic approach comes from a chaotic home where fighting, abandonment, and other serious issues are presented almost daily. Needless to say, his approach to handling his problems was in much the same manner as that modeled for him by his family. One day he became explosive and literally tore the entire room up. He dumped out buckets of crayons, tore pages from books, turned over desks, and threw chairs. You name it, he did it—and all with a smile on his face. The teacher, recognizing that she must get the children out of the classroom, removes the children and calls me down to handle this out-of-control child. He calms down, we talk about how we are going to fix this, and plan for a repayment of the grief that he has caused. Within a day or so, he decided to try the destructive approach again in his reading class. At this time, his teachers met and we came up with a plan of action to help this child learn from this experience. Each teacher knew the role that she would play in executing this plan. One teacher explained (with tons of love) that he had the opportunity of a lifetime to help repay for the damages done and the energy that had been drained. By the time she was finished, he was convinced that he was the luckiest kid in the whole school and that he was going to have the opportunity to work in the cafeteria during his break times to clean windows and sweep under tables. I, the counselor, was the supervisor who loaded him up with empathy, encouragement, and reinforcing statements that sent the "Can Do" message. The janitor even played his part. He came up with a loving yet firm voice telling this young man what he needed him to do and how he expected the windows and floors to look when finished. He even checked on him periodically and generally told him that he was doing a fine job. (Talk about a face light-up.) His homeroom teacher kept her loving role by offering tons of empathy. Not one single lecture came from her mouth.

The amazing ending to this story is that the boy had such a sense of self-worth that he had cleaned these windows as repayment. He seldom uses anger to solve his problems now. The greatest thing is this: after he came back to the room that he had destroyed, he wrote the teacher a letter of apology and began to cry as he told her about missing his dad and hating the divorce that his parents are going through. His reading teacher, at this time, was empathetic and encouraged him to write a book about his feelings. He became excited about the idea and has started a book about how kids feel about divorce. He said, "I want to write this so other kids will know that there are others out there that have the same feelings." Wow! This hit every teacher involved. Would lecturing or scolding have brought out the true feelings of this little guy? Would time-outs or loss of privileges have brought about this bonding experience between him and his teachers? No, only Love and Logic can do that. This is probably the only time this child has had a safe, loving way of handling a problem demonstrated for him.

Another few tidbits of Love and Logic fun around here. I had a teacher come to me and exclaim, "Johnny (a second-grader) isn't doing his work again today, and I am so excited." I oddly looked at her. I have never had a teacher say with a smile on her face that she was excited that a child wasn't doing his work. She explained that she had talked to the mother and they had come up with a plan to help this little guy realize that doing his work at school is much more fun and profitable for him. She told me that teaching was much more relaxing since she didn't have to worry about laying down immediate consequences. Her carefully laid out plans were more to the benefit of the child also. She has a lot of practice opportunities for her classroom. She says that she is down to only three children who need to practice occasionally. She tells them that they are the luckiest class in the school to get these practice opportunities, and you know she is right!

One last fun thing (can't tell them all to you). Our teachers are becoming energy-drain experts around here. One day a little boy's mother came to me quite tickled at her son's remedy for his teacher's reoccurring energy problems. The family had been discussing at the dinner table the food groups and those that are best for energy (the older sister is in sports). The next day, when the teacher was very sad because another energy drain had occurred, Elic (a second-grader) raised his hand politely and with great concern said, "Mrs. Pingleton, maybe you would have more energy if you ate more bread." We have a lot more fun around here these days.

SINCERELY,
LISA PHILLIPS

Some mornings, my son, Marcus, and daughter, Royelle, would have trouble finding all of their things. I use to help them search for everything. Then one day I realized that I was giving them "losing" lessons, so I created a plan. The next time Marcus couldn't find his sneakers, instead of helping him look for them, I just said, "Let's go." We left home with out his sneakers. When we got to camp, I explained to the counselor what had happened.

After I left, the counselor told Marcus that, since he did not have his sneakers, he would have to stay inside that day.

To this day, Marcus always knows where both of his shoes are. And I get to work on time.

MARY FLOYD

My sister-in-law, a teacher, told me about the book she had just read, *Teaching with Love and Logic.* My first thoughts were, "No discipline—it won't work." After giving it more thought, I asked her for a catalog. After all, the discipline I use wasn't working in my home. Reluctantly, but willing to try a new parenting technique, I ordered a *Love and Logic Starter Package.*

After listening to *Helicopters, Drill Sergeants, and Consultants* and reading the *Love and Logic Journal* (vol. 17, no. 2), I put into practice the next morning what I had just learned. I said to my two oldest daughters, ages ten and eight, "I will be available to take you to the birthday party when all of your Saturday chores are done. We need to leave at 1:00 if you don't want to be late." Typically, my daughters would come to me at 1:00 and ask me to drive them to the party even though their clothes were still in the dryer, promising me they would finish the chore when they got home. And typically, I would drive them to the party lecturing them and telling them that if they had started their laundry earlier and spent less time playing in their room and more time cleaning it, then everything would have been done on time and I wouldn't be so mad. But this was not a typical day, because this was the first day I used Love and Logic. To my sweet surprise, my two daughters had finished all their chores early, with two hours to spare!

Wow, this really works! It was too easy! I was kind of hoping they would mess up so that they could learn a lesson. But I now know that life gives us many opportunities to learn from. I am so happy they will now be able to learn so much at such young ages. Thanks so much! I feel so much better knowing that I am not responsible for their every move.

After driving my older daughters to the party, I took my two younger daughters, ages six and five, to run errands with me. My youngest is notorious for running away from me, right to the edge of parking lots. She does this just to hear me yell, "Julia, *stop!*" She also likes to play "find me" in stores. Spankings have never worked with her.

Our first stop was the mall. Before we got out of the car I said, "Children who stay with their mom in the parking lot and at the mall might get a treat at the end of the day." No problems at the mall. The next stop was the library. Again I said, "Children who stay with their mom in the parking lot and in the library might get a treat at the end of the day." No problems at the library. I repeated the same line again before we went into the craft store. And again, no problems.

What would usually have been a very stressful day was actually a very enjoyable day (for all of us). My favorite part was when I told my two younger daughters how proud I was of them and the choices that they had made. Then I said to them, "All of my errands are done but I have another choice for you to make, do you want to go home or get some ice cream?"

What a beautiful day! Just think, this was my very first day using the Love and Logic parenting technique! I can't wait for tomorrow and more opportunities for my children to grow and become more responsible. It's amazing what happened when I told my two older daughters what *I* was going to do, instead of telling them over and over what I wanted them to do. It was also nice having my two younger daughters think about a possible treat instead of thinking about how to upset me. Thank you so much! I look forward to reading *Parenting with Love and Logic* tonight!

ANN MCCAULEY

I came home the other day and discovered my daughter's bicycle in the driveway. Luckily it was not in my way or there would have been natural consequences a little sooner than I expected. When I walked in I immediately said to my daughter, "Shelby, there is something so sad in the driveway." As soon as she heard the word "sad" she knew something was up. Shelby asked what was so sad. I replied, "Your bicycle is in the driveway. Would you like to put it away or pay me to do it for you?" Shelby, being as clever as she is, says, "How much are you going to charge me?" Well, I was stumped at first, so I told her that I'd get back to her on the price.

I then asked her what she thought might happen if no one picked up her bike. Shelby said that it would probably get run over. I agreed with her. I then asked what she thought might happen to her bike if it got run over. Shelby thought for a moment and then said, "The frame would get bent and the tire too!" I turned to my husband and asked, "How much would it cost to fix the frame and replace the tire?" He said, "About $25." I said to Shelby, "Well, that's the price for picking it up for you—$25." Shelby immediately said, "Ah! It's not worth it. I'll go pick it up." Her bike hasn't been left out since.

CHRIS BLACKMAN

My ten-year-old daughter was packing only a piece of fruit, a drink, and a dessert for lunch. Monday I told her she was not making appropriate lunches (she knows what that means) and I would be making her lunch. I packed her a beautiful sardine sandwich. That evening she said nothing about her lunch. When I asked how it was, she replied, "Moooooom, you forgot my drink!" I had to leave the room to compose myself. When I returned I asked how her sandwich was. She replied, "The salmon had bones in it. Next time can you remove the bones and leave off the bread?" Thinking I needed to work on my action plan, I again made her lunch on Tuesday, this time packing a cold hot dog. That evening she told me I forgot her dessert and I had not packed her snack all week (gee, didn't know I was supposed to). Tuesday night before bed, she packed her own lunch and snack and asked that I check to make sure it was okay.

Wow! With no lecturing, no nagging, no telling her what she was supposed to learn, she decided to do it herself.

Thanks. Love and Logic has taken so much stress out of my life. I can enjoy my kids so much more because I don't have to be a mother hen— just a loving mom raising responsible kids.

CINDY STANLEY

I'd just finished a Love and Logic class, sponsored by my local school district. It was great. I couldn't wait to try some things out. I got my chance last night, it was so fun.

We had asked our four- and six-year-old boys, Steve and Trey, to clean the upstairs playroom, it was a disaster. You really could not get from one end of the room to the other, and not even close to the bookcase. They immediately started the usual complaints: "It's too much!" "It will take too long!" "How come the girls don't have to help?" "I don't want to!"

This is how it played out from there:

MOM: Well, you can get it done before bedtime, or you can do it first thing in the morning. What would you like to do?

TREY: In the morning.

MOM: Okay, when does morning start?

TREY: At eight.

MOM: No, that's not right, want to guess again?...No...Need some help?...(nodding his head, yes)...Morning starts at 12:01 A.M.

TREY: What?! I'm not getting up at 12:01!

MOM: Well you still have another choice, you could still get it done before bedtime.

TREY: No, I'll do it in the morning, but morning is not 12:01!

MOM: Okay Trey, good night, see you in the morning.

I set my alarm for 11:55 and woke them up at 12:01. My two groggy and cranky little boys complained and cried *while* I led them up to the playroom. And continued to complain and cry while they picked up toys and books and stuff off the floor. And once in a while, they would stop and say, "I'm not doing any more!" Where I would reply, "Oh, that's sad, I can start helping again when you start picking up again." Of course I got, "I'm too tired!" I just kept my cool and didn't say, "Well, if you had done it earlier you wouldn't be here." Instead I said, "Oh, I know, you can go back to bed as soon as you are done." I don't know how many times I said that, but it was quite a few.

When the room was clean and ready to vacuum, I let them go back to bed, tucked them in, and waited by the closed door for moment, to make sure all was well. I heard them talking: "Steve, what do you think of *that?!* I guess we better not do that anymore." "Yeah, I don't like to get up *first thing in the morning!*" "And know what, Steve, maybe we better not waste any more food either, I heard her talking to Janice about that, and you know food costs a lot of money." "Yeah, Trey."

I went back to bed with a smile on my face. My lucky little boys learned something, *and* the room got clean. *And* it was so much fun. I am excited to practice more Love and Logic on my children.

CORI WRIGHT

You know you have Love and Logic kids if the kids (four-year-old daughter and six-year-old son) are in bed, while Mom and I are enjoying a relaxing snuggle, and suddenly there's a huge crash followed by lots giggles. I say, "Uh-oh!" and the kids say, "What's wrong?" My reply, "Our agreement is you guys can stay up as late as you want as long as we don't see you or hear you, and I just heard you. Do you want to pay me back in cash or chores?" "Chores!" both kids chorus happily. Then my daughter says, "Daddy, can my chore be to clean the toilets and the bathrooms please?" I tried to say "Sure," but before I could get that out, my son starts in with, "No! I want to do the toilets!" As they start the debate, all I can get out is, "Well, I'm sure you two will figure it out and if you can't decide, I'll decide in the morning." I return to the master bedroom to find my wife doubled over in laughter. Love and Logic parenting is so much fun!

RICK RADDATZ

I am beginning my third year teaching the *Becoming a Love and Logic Parent* program and would like to share a success story about my son.

When Tony began elementary school, I found that he would often come home with a long face. "Why the long face?" I'd ask, and he always seemed to reply that he wasn't good at something, or someone else was better than he was. The standard answer, "Oh, but you're good at other things they're not good at," just didn't seem to work.

Then I learned about the "I Notice" routine and "Attribution Theory" and started using them consistently. He perked up when I'd notice something about him, and I gave him heavy doses of encouragement, trying to be as specific as I could about what I saw and letting him make his own judgment.

On his schoolwork, I asked him to pick out his best paper and tell me about it. My favorite phrase became, "How did you *do* that?!" Someone had said that to me when I was a child and I still remember the pride I felt. (Another reminder that the things we do and say will stick with kids for the rest of their lives!) I found that as I modeled consistently recognizing his strengths, Tony began to do the same. He seemed to stop dwelling on his weaknesses and the long-face days dropped way down.

It didn't happen overnight; it took about two years. But the moment came when my heart melted and I knew I'd made a difference. Tony and his father came home from an errand, and my husband reported that in the middle of their conversation, Tony's eyes widened with a sudden realization, "Gee, Dad, I'm good at a *lot* of things!" Yes! He got it!

DeAnn Dickinson

Dear Jim Fay,

I wanted to write and tell you how Love and Logic has made a difference in our family. We have been following this program for a number of years.

Our oldest son is particularly influenced by money. He had lost his second pair of gloves early in the winter season, so I knew I had the perfect opportunity to implement a Jim Fay-ism. The day he came home and told me he lost his gloves, I looked into his eyes and said, "How sad, what are you going to do?" He responded, "I've looked in the lost and found and they're not there."

The next morning as I kissed him goodbye I kissed his hands too and he said, "What's that for?" I said, "I thought your hands might need some extra love to keep them warm, and have a nice day." Day number two—and still no gloves at the lost and found. I decided to step in and offer the "Would you like to hear what some other kids have tried?" line. He took me up on the rental suggestion. He would rent gloves from me for 75¢ each day and if he lost these gloves it would really be a bummer. He agreed and rented the gloves that day and for one more day after that. He began to add up what it would cost to rent the gloves for the entire winter and was determined to find his gloves. Well, divine intervention struck on day number five. He came home from school with a smile and said, "You'll never guess what happened! I went to the lost and found again just like every day and there were my gloves!"

He happily paid his rental fee and said he wouldn't be needing the service anymore. To date he's lost no gloves!

LIVING THE LOVE AND LOGIC WAY!
DEBBI KOPPIN

As everyone knows it is very exciting to send your first child off to kindergarten. Everyone wants to see what their "baby" learned on the their first day. What I didn't realize is that I was making myself a new job as I made it my responsibility to empty out our son Logan's backpack every day. This continued through kindergarten and I really enjoyed it.

Then first grade rolled around. At the first parent-teacher conference we learned that the kids were going to be bringing books home to be read and it was important that they be returned the next day for the next child to read. That really got me stuck with the backpack-checking job. Logan does not like reading. He would rather be playing ruff and tuff with his four little brothers. Every night I would be after him to get his book read, his sentences done, everything packed into his backpack, and the backpack ready by the door. One morning he left his backpack on the chair and I had to run out to the truck before Logan and his dad left for the bus stop. That's when I started thinking about Logan's backpack this year, and all his little brothers' backpacks forever and endlessly for the rest of my life. I'd finally had enough!

First, I wrote a letter to the Love and Logic Institute, asking about how to hire Jim Fay to come talk at our school and train parents and teachers on Love and Logic techniques. Next, I wrote a note to Logan's teacher, telling her that Logan might be coming to school with books unread, maybe no books at all, and possibly not even his backpack. I asked if she would please keep him in from recess if he forgot to bring his books. I told her that it should not become a problem for her; if she needed to do errands or something, it was okay to have Logan sit quietly without books in the library with his head down—anything she thought appropriate. I asked her to put a hand on his shoulder and be sad for him; that way he couldn't be mad at her, only at himself for making a bad decision.

Now I was getting excited! Logan is a very mild-tempered child, so this was our first chance at a training session. Monday night was the best night of a year and a half of schooling. There was no scolding, no hollering, and no worries. I asked him only one question. "Are you going to read those books tonight or at 5:30 in the morning or would you rather not read them at all?" "I'll read in the morning," he decided. "Okay, goodnight," I replied.

I heard his alarm go off for five minutes on Tuesday morning, then knock-knock, "Mom, will you get up and listen to me read?" "Gee, I'd love to, Logan, but I'm way too tired." He was mad; he whined and stomped all the way downstairs. Bummer, but he got his books read. Same story on Wednesday: up again at 5:30 reading his books. But that morning he informed his dad that he'd be reading his books before bed from now on. Fine with us, he's reading and returning the books, I'm not yelling any-more. He got to choose when, and if he forgot, the teacher was in on the plan. Problem solved, we have a more responsible kid. He didn't even have to miss a recess to learn! All was well, until…

One morning a few days later, my husband, Joel, was loaded down with a lunchbox, water jug, thermoses, and coffee cups. He and Logan were walking out to the truck when he noticed that Logan didn't have his backpack, so he said, "Boy, I sure get tired of carrying all this stuff every day. Maybe since you're not carrying anything, you can help me?" He told me that Logan took about four steps and said, "Dad! I forgot my backpack. Should I run and get it?" Dad said, "Sure, but I hope I'm still here by the time you get back!" Which goes to show you, even dads are softies, giving reminders on the sly like that!

DEE WILLIAMSON

❧

Dear Jim,

I heard you speak yesterday in my hometown of Grand Rapids, Michigan, and it inspired me to write down one of my own Love and Logic stories and send it to you. This is a story that I tell when we are discussing the concepts of "Thinking Words" and "Enforceable Statements" in the seminars I teach.

Summer days in Michigan can be very hot and humid. I awoke to just such a day. As the kids stumbled downstairs for breakfast I suggested to them that we do all of our jobs in the morning, and then go swimming at a neighbor's pool. This sounded like an ideal plan to me, but the kids were not enthused. As I whipped through my chores, they groused around and did absolutely nothing—in spite of all my encouraging words. Finally I caved in to the inevitable and announced to them that swimming was for people whose jobs were done, and since they had not done any we would not be going swimming that day. Boy, was I bummed. They did not seem to care very much, and probably even thought that they had gotten out of doing their usual chores.

By the time my husband arrived on the scene at 5:30, I had progressed from frustrated to downright discouraged. I told him the sad story of the day and how I felt like Love and Logic principles had not worked for me—for the first time ever! Then inspiration struck. I walked over to the kitchen window and made an announcement to the kids, who were playing in the backyard: "Dinner is ready for everybody whose jobs are done." My son didn't quite catch what I had said, so my husband repeated it to him. "Oh," said my son, "I guess I'd better go pick up some dog doo." Our two daughters came zooming through the kitchen on their way upstairs, to make beds and pick up dirty clothes. They were shortly followed by our son. By this time my husband and I had decided that, since our jobs were done, we would begin eating our own dinner. I must confess that we were enjoying this scenario so much that we could not resist the urge to call after them, "We'll try to save you something." We had the most pleasant meal we'd had in weeks, which seemed to increase our appetites considerably. When the children did manage to join us I did not jump up from my meal to serve them. Instead I said, "The vegetables are on the stove, and here is what's left of the salad." It was probably the most fun we'd had disciplining our kids in years. Thanks, Love and Logic!

And thanks, Jim, for all you do to make parenting a joy. I really enjoyed your talks at Forest Hills High School. After teaching the *Becoming a Love and Logic Parent* program for eight years and watching your videos repeatedly, you feel like a member of the family.

Sincerely,
Helen Milanowski

At one of my Love and Logic training sessions, a mother shared the following story. Her nine-year-old son, "Dan," is the most challenging of their five children. Dan creates a tension in the air wherever he is. One day while riding in the family's twelve-passenger van, Dan's tension reached out and touched his brother like a bolt of lightning. The next thing Mom saw in the rearview mirror was pushing, shoving, and things being thrown over the seats. Well, Mom had to stop the van and get control of this situation. The verbal battle began—"He did it first!" etc. We all know the verbal tennis match that kids can play with us. Mom just decided to order one brother to sit up front, and Dan to take the seat in the last row. Separate the combatants…each fighter sit in your corner and wait for the bell to begin the next round. Haven't we all been through this as parents with our children…feeling like a referee…losing control! Well, Mom got the children safely to their destinations.

A few days later, Mom had to take Dan to one of his special activities, which he really enjoyed. This time it was just Mom and Dan in the large commuter van. Mom got in the driver's seat; Dan got in the seat right behind her with a great view out the front windshield. Mom thought to herself, "Dan's supposed to sit in the last seat for the next week as a consequence for his disruptive behavior with his brother, but he's peaceful now, I'm peaceful: he's a lovable kid."

The courageous moment has arrived for Mom: "Should I let the consequence slide this time, or do I have the courage to follow through and make my words gold?" Sometimes as parents it seems easier to take the path of least resistance. But this mother took a deep breath of courage and told her son that he had to go to the back of the van. Can't you just imagine the response from Dan? "This is not fair! This doesn't make sense! Aw, Mom, no one else is going to know!" To each verbal attempt to manipulate with those simple words, Mom replied with the "Brain Dead" response: "I know."

Well, Dan was ready to win this battle so he announced, "I'm not going to the back of the van!" Mom, breathing in more courage and using the things she had been learning in her Love and Logic training, turned to Dan with the "Sympathy" technique: "That's so sad—the van is not going to your activity until you are in the seat where you belong." Mom waited quietly with more courage. Dan got up, mumbling under his breath, "It's not fair," and went to the back of the van, took his seat, and buckled his seatbelt. Mom asked, "Are you ready, Dan?" He replied, "I guess so."

The trip was quiet, but the real payoff was that over the next week Mom did not have to ask Dan one time to go to the back of the van and take his seat. He did so all on his own without verbal battles. Things continued to be calmer with Dan and the other children when traveling with Mom in the van.

All parents face situations similar to this with their children. Having the courage to follow through faces us all. The next time you face a situation like this, remember to breathe in the spirit of courage and follow through. The lesson learned by the child is a real deposit in the bank account of life.

JIM NICHOLSON

Both of our older children get regular practice tidying up the playroom. They are really good at making a mess and even better at avoiding the cleaning. Since the playroom belongs to our children, we do not get too involved in how it looks. It is in the lower level of our house and, thankfully, we don't need to walk through it for too many things.

When the room gets really messy the two older kids say things like, "Can we please play in the kitchen or the living room?" At which time I say, "Feel free to play in there when the playroom is clean."

This strategy worked fine until we had another baby, who as a toddler would avoid the playroom because he didn't want to hurt his feet. Well at this point, my patience for a hurricane in the playroom began to wear thin and was compounded when the older kids chose to watch TV rather than clean up.

I needed another strategy, so I went back to my Love and Logic parenting materials and was reminded to model what to do without telling the kids what to do. So when I was working on a project, I would say things like, "I think I'll put away [this] before I start [that] so I don't have so much to pick up." And I wouldn't say a thing to them about what they should learn. Even when they chose to turn on the TV, I would only say things like, "Feel free to leave the TV on as long as I can't hear it up here." They would look at me in utter amazement, as if they did it so that I would tell them to turn the TV off and then that would become the issue.

This went on for a couple of months. Every time the playroom would succumb to a hurricane, I would go into my "Feel free to..." mode.

Then one day at the completion of a three-day pickup session, our six-year-old said a profound thing: "Mom, I think I'm just going to get out one thing at a time and then pick it up before I get out something else."

I was amazed, and somehow in a split second I thought of how this lesson would have looked had I told him what to do instead, so I said, "How do you think that might work for you?" And he said, "Good." Oh the wisdom!

JODI JACOBSON

I just started subscribing to the *Love and Logic Journal*. It's been eleven years since I first heard your tapes and this absence of support is starting to show in my parenting style. I laughed my way through the journal and realized what I have been missing. It's been tough work doing it "my way."

I have three boys, Jake (thirteen), Jackson (five), and Carson (twenty-one months). Ever since Carson was born, I have struggled to keep Jackson quiet during Carson's naptime. Jackson would routinely raise his voice (and then claim he "forgot" that Carson was asleep). Worse, he would throw vigorous and unending tantrums. You can imagine all the "punishments" I tried to motivate him to keep quiet. Nothing worked, and *I* was ready to take a nap!

When I read my first issue of the *Love and Logic Journal,* the Love and Logic wheels in my brain started spinning again. When Jackson gave me another chance to offer meaningful consequences, I was ready. I calmly explained that if his loud voice woke up Carson, he would be very tired and would need to go to bed early. Whatever time Carson went to bed would be Jackson's bedtime as well.

I'm pleased to say that Jackson tested this immediately and that night went to bed at the same time as his younger brother. As I tucked him in, he said, "Mom, tomorrow I'm going to be quiet during Carson's nap." Victory!

JULIE WHEATCROFT

Last spring Caitlin came home from her second-grade class and shook a paper in my face! She said, "Mom, look at this! This is an L&L Paper!" ("L&L" is what she calls Love and Logic). I took the paper and said, "Caitlin, this looks like a math sheet." Caitlin smirked and said, "I *know* what it looks like but this is an L&L math paper. Our teacher told us we were going to have math homework and then she said, 'Don't do all the problems, that's too many! You can either do the odd ones or the even ones!' Well, I knew what she was trying to do; that is that Love and Logic stuff. I am gonna show her that stuff doesn't work with me!"

Trying not to smile, I asked Caitlin what she meant. She was already stomping down the hall but she called back to me, "I am gonna show that teacher how I feel about L&L. I'm gonna *do all those math problems* and see how she likes that!" I was glad she was in her room by that time, because I had to sit down on the couch and have a hearty laugh.

The next morning I asked Caitlin about her math sheet and she proudly showed me that all the problems had been done. Caitlin said, "I can't wait to see how my teacher acts when I show her." I told her I couldn't wait either! After school I asked her what her teacher had done and Caitlin smiled and said, "Mom, she was so surprised! I told her that L&L stuff doesn't work on me and she smiled and said, 'Guess not.'"

KELLY SMITH

I am a mom to three wonderful stepkids, two boys, ages ten and eleven, and a girl, age seven, and to a fantastic son, age eight. My husband and I got married in June 1999. At the time, the kids were running wild. I was told stories of kids who literally jumped on furniture, ran all over the house, screamed, cursed, hit, kicked, and fought with each other constantly. I saw for myself how they treated their parents, especially their father. If he told them to stop they would start screaming at him, cursing at him, telling him that he didn't love them and that they hated him—even going so far as to hit him and run away from him.

My sister-in-law told me of an incident where my oldest stepson got in trouble and when his father tried to talk to him, he ran out of the house into the pouring rain, into the woods behind her house, and his father ran after him, spent thirty minutes chasing him, finally dragging him back into the house, at which time the child locked himself in the bathroom and refused to come out for over an hour. (My reaction was, "Why did he run after him?")

As the kids got more familiar with my authority, I began to change things. When the kids fought, I would tell them that the fighting hurt my ears and tell them that they were free to return to the family room when they were finished. When we were out somewhere and they started acting up, I would end the outing. When we played a game and someone would start whining or crying that something was "unfair," the game would end immediately. When one of the kids used a rude word, name, or obscenity, I very sweetly told them that since they found that word so interesting, they could write it twenty-five, fifty, or one hundred times—or if it was a word that actually meant something, they got to write the definition too! When they were told to do something (a chore, etc.) and started whining,

I told them I couldn't understand them when they talked like that, and when they started arguing that kids "shouldn't have to do chores" and that "it's the mom's job to do all that stuff," I explained calmly that if I had to pick up all the toys and vacuum all the floors, etc., then I wouldn't have time to take them to the park, movies, or some other fun activity. When my stepdaughter threw a temper tantrum in our living room, I led her outside and said, "When you are finished, you are welcome to come back in." (You should have seen the look on her face.) The first few times, she would stand on our front porch and scream for ten to fifteen minutes, trying to see if we were going to react.

When the oldest stepchild moved in with us, he was having major problems in school (and had been for over two years)—he'd been suspended for fighting, he'd had many detentions for physical altercations and refusal to do homework, and two schools had suggested having him repeat different grades; he was also having serious problems with his siblings—fighting and even threatening his brother and another peer with a knife (two separate incidents) and had little respect for any authority figure. When he refused to do homework, I gave him the consequence of no TV or video games—if he did his work, he had limited time for that day; if he missed a homework assignment, he had no time that day. We had many weeks of no TV time and he tried everything under the sun—bargaining (which was ignored), screaming and yelling (which was responded to with a request to return when he was quieter), and simple sullenness (which was simply not responded to!). This year he has yet to miss a homework assignment!

As my husband noticed the kids responding to me and listening to what I said, he started following my lead. We gradually saw improvements in their interactions with us, others, and each other. We still had work to do. (One of the things that bothered me was when I'd make a meal and the kids would take one look and moan, groan, and do the "*Eeeewwww! That is gross!* Yuck!" thing. My response was to remove their plate from the table and say, "Goodbye, I hope you like breakfast better," and then excuse them from the table. After missing a few meals, and a discussion as to what was an appropriate expression of their feelings, they started saying things like, "I really do not like that, can I make myself a sandwich?" (this approach also worked well for food fights, hiding food, and refusing to use table manners), but we were making progress!

It has been three years, and the oldest stepchild now lives with us and has made massive improvements—he is doing well in school (he is not making straight A's, but he is working up to his ability and he is proud of himself), he has positive self-esteem, he has friends, and he is happy. That he is happy and proud of himself in and of itself is *such* an accomplishment. I doubt we'd have been as successful if we had not used Love and Logic, so thank you. Thank you very much.

CHRIS NOECKER-DONMOYER

My son *loves* his Legos. He loves playing with them all night long in his room by the glow of the hall light. Sometimes I find him in the morning asleep on the floor with a Lego imprint on his forehead. The only problem with him staying up late is that he wants to sleep late in the morning and that throws my schedule off. So I bought an alarm clock. We made a deal that he could stay up as long as he wanted—but wakeup time is 7:00 A.M. The next morning the alarm clock is ringing and my son is lying in his bed, dead to the world, snoring away. I wake him up with some progressively more active shaking of his leg. Finally he's semiconscious and he says, "I'm tiiiiiired Daaaaady." I give him some empathy—I say, "I understand. I'm always sleepy if I stay up too late." Being the Love and Logic kid he is, he asks, "What do some other kids do?" Starting with the bad options first, I say, "Well, some other sleepy kids get out of bed and run as fast as they can into the wall. *Smack!* How do you think that would work?" He cringes in his semisleep and says, "Ouch Daddy! That would hurt! I don't want to do that!" So I continue, "Well, some other sleepy kids get out of bed and stick their head in the toilet and blow bubbles. How do you think that would work?" He says, "*Yuck* Daddy! I don't want to do that. What else do kids do?" Then I close the deal. "Some other kids decide not to stay up so late if they have to get up at 7 A.M. How do you think that would work?" He replies with a very smart thing for a six-year-old: "I think that's a very good idea, Dad."

RICK RADDATZ

Six months ago I wrote a story about my son and learning responsibility. Being the mother of three children, completing the story was not my first priority. The amazing thing is what has taken place since I wrote the original story. It is a classic example of how powerful Love and Logic is in teaching kids responsibility in a loving way.

My son John has had the opportunity of spending time with very loving and well-meaning adults at daycare and preschool for the last four years. However, in their need to be good care-givers he has learned that adults worry about picking up toys, not him. His first baby-sitter treated him like an honored guest and spent naptime cleaning up after the kids. She also complained a lot about what a mess he had made, when I picked him up. I always felt like she babied him and had low expectations of him, but I believed that as long as he was happy while he was there, that was all that mattered. His current baby-sitter is very loving and well meaning but she uses the technique of balancing loving limits with nagging.

John was born prematurely and as a result has had ongoing respiratory problems that have caused him to deal with a lot of medications and breathing treatments at a very young age. In this area of his life, I was very empathetic with him and as a result, he had learned to deal with these tough things well. Yet when asked to do something he didn't want to do, he could have temper tantrums better than anyone I know.

Ten months ago we had our third child. My maternity leave has given me the opportunity to practice what I know about good parenting, full-time, without any "help" from daycare. Because John had been so lovingly enabled, he has become a master at the art of dawdling. He can avoid picking up better than almost anyone I know. I learned while living with him all day every day that when I was working, the picking up I did at night or leaving his toys out in the living room rather than having him be accountable was denying him the most valuable opportunity to learn. At the time I thought it was better to pick my battles with him after a long day at work. However, I have learned that, while picking battles carefully, Love and Logic parents don't like to feel bad, so they take action to share the responsibility so that life is a win/win situation.

Well, after many days of looking at the disaster on the living room floor and no luck in speeding up the pickup process, I asked John if he wanted to pick the toys up before bed or before breakfast the next day. He replied, "Before breakfast," with a smug kind of tone that sounded a lot like no problem for him. My recall of Love and Logic was now in overdrive.

You see, I continue to work hard to replace my innate reactions from my forebrain (anger, threats, and warnings) with empathy and smiles. My parents have had an incredible ability for unconditional love. In fact, I credit this asset of mine to them. No matter how bad we were, my brothers and I knew they loved us. However, they used a lot of warnings and whining to get my brothers and me to do what we needed to do—and you can probably imagine how well that went over. Thankfully, after much personal struggle as young adults, my brothers and I turned out to be okay. It is the personal struggle as a young adult that I hope my children can live as toddlers and young children when the consequences are much smaller.

With my knowledge of Love and Logic in overdrive, I tucked him in bed with a big hug and kiss and began to plan how not to react the next morning when he didn't clean up. Well, I was prepared, because I felt like I had dreamt Love and Logic all night long.

When John woke up, the first thing he said was that he wanted cereal for breakfast. I gently reminded him of our conversation from the night before and said that I would be happy to discuss breakfast with him when he finished picking up. He still had that smug look as he walked into the living room and sat on the floor. His sister finished her breakfast and sat down to watch TV. He watched too. When I came into the room, he smiled at me and I smiled back.

About midmorning, I told the kids that we would be leaving soon to do some errands. John, being the "keeper" he is, said, "What about my breakfast?" I asked him if he had finished picking up his toys. The word "no" was barely audible amongst the sobbing.

I felt so bad, but kept telling myself that the lessons he was learning for the long run would more than make up for this little bit of pain on my part. I also remembered something, which is the cornerstone of Love and Logic, which seemed to give my guilt some relief for the moment. Now was the time to lock in the learning with empathy. So I said to John, "It's okay honey, the good thing is, we will finish our errands and come right home and eat lunch." "But I'll be hungry," he moaned. "I bet you will," I said, followed by, "What do you think we should eat for lunch?"

That statement caused him to stop crying long enough to get into the car and leave. As we pulled out of the driveway, he said a very profound thing: "Next time I guess I shouldn't make such a mess."

When we got home, I told him I would be happy to discuss lunch with him as soon as he finished picking up. He wasn't very thrilled, but he didn't throw himself on the floor. And I saw something never seen before in our house, a child picking up with lightning speed. Well, I thought I had really done a great job because he had really seemed to learn a wonderful lesson about making a mess and cleaning it up. Then that night, as we finished dinner, I asked John if he would be picking up his toys before bedtime or before breakfast, and he said, with a smile, "Before breakfast." The next morning, when he told me what he wanted for breakfast, I reminded him of his choice and he said, "Oh no, not this again!" But instead of throwing himself on the floor, he proceeded to pick up a little faster than the morning before.

This proved to be day two of many days of learning. And he is still learning, but his decisions are much wiser and now he says things like, "I am such a good cleaner" and "Mom, I made such a big mess in my room and I'll be picking it up before I go outside to play." He still plays with his toys and picks them up and he still needs limits in order to keep the situation from getting out of hand, but now within those limits he is the fastest and happiest cleaner I know.

Parents learn a lot in this process too. I have noticed that it is a lot easier for me to smile and speak with lilt in my voice when my own kids are making big decisions because I am so confident that I have a way of helping them learn from their mistakes, without making the problem my own.

JODI JACOBSON

My son, seven, was apparently a little wild last week during a daycamp field trip. When my husband picked the kids up at the end of the day, he was told that Andy would not be able to attend this week's field trip unless he or I accompanied him. The alternative was to spend the day at the pre-school-aged daycare.

My first thought (okay my second thought, my first thought was an angry one!) was that I'd work from home that day and just keep him there with me. Then I remembered the Love and Logic tapes and realized what a learning opportunity this was for my son. So, this morning, my husband took my daughter to daycamp, all ready to spend the day at the Royals game. I took my son to the preschool. This was not fun. I almost had to carry him inside, he was hyperventilating, more tears than I've ever seen. It took everything I had not to give in and take him home with me. I kept hearing those tapes in my mind! I managed not to cry until I left the building.

When I picked my son up at the end of the day, he told me, "I got a new attitude, Mama," and we have definitely seen signs of improvement! I'm pretty sure he's learned quite a lesson about behavior today—and that we won't back down just because he's unhappy with the repercussions of his behavior.

MANDY GAULDIN

I live in a beautiful town in southern Utah. There are many wonderful parents there who try with all their heart to do the right thing for their families. Nevertheless, frustrations and difficulties arise. I remember one beautiful young mother in one of my recent classes. Her name is Lynn. She has two sons, ages seven and eleven, and a three-year-old daughter. She expressed, at the beginning of the *Becoming a Love and Logic Parent* classes, that she couldn't control her children without yelling, threatening, and getting really upset. She dreaded coming home after work because she didn't want to fight with them to get daily necessities done. She said that her husband, John, seemed to have very little problem getting the children to do what he asked. John is an easygoing, sweet-mannered man and Lynn was beside herself.

She did not feel in control. She didn't want to discipline like her father—with an iron fist. She remembers having a happy childhood and she said she couldn't ever remember doing really anything disobedient as a child. Lynn remembers never being able to make decisions on her own because her parents were rather overprotective. She stated that she felt like she didn't do a whole lot "right." She remembers not even being allowed to load the dishwasher because she was shown she couldn't do it correctly. Consequently, she was shy and was condescending to her "Drill Sergeant" father.

She wanted her family to be different. She, too, wanted to be loving and kind like her husband, yet teach her children what they needed to know to grow to be responsible adults. She wanted to enjoy her children in the process of their growing years. She wanted her children to think back to their childhood with fondness and appreciation. I assured her that the stress would be less in a couple of weeks and the control level would be much higher. She promised me she would study and read and call me if she needed to. We talked about the most difficult time—mornings. Others in the class helped with ideas. It was a group effort, not just a teacher-to-student solution. We brainstormed with different Love and Logic tools and she had not only ideas to take home, but also support if things got too rough for her.

Each week she returned with hope and resolve to continue learning. She asked wonderful questions and was a diligent student of the *Becoming a Love and Logic Parent* program. Lynn shared with the group the story of her oldest son going deer hunting with his dad. Her son didn't want to wear his jacket. The "old" Lynn would have insisted. The new "Love and Logic" Lynn gave him a choice of packing it or carrying it. He chose to carry it to the car, but during the hunt with his father he refused to wear the coat. Lynn said that he absolutely froze during that time and her son shyly reported back to Mom that she was right, he will definitely take his coat next time and wear it! She reported back to us that knowing Love and Logic principles allowed the consequences to do the teaching. What a wonderful learning opportunity for their son.

On the evening of the last class, Lynn was relaxed and reported that she'd had not only a happy week with her kids, but that she'd had a less stressful one as well. When I asked her if she thought the classes were worth taking the time to attend, she smiled and said, "Oh yes, they were really worth it!"

MARTI LINDQUIST

My husband and I have been practicing Love and Logic techniques in our home for three years. We have two daughters, ages seven and eleven. I've felt that we've had a lot of success with Love and Logic and those feelings were confirmed by the following conversations I recently had with Jenny, the eleven-year-old.

My girls were debating the pros and cons of Love and Logic. Jenny indicated that she really likes being able to make her own decisions. In her words, "When I make a good choice, I feel really good about it and when I make a bad choice…" She paused and thought a moment, then continued. "Well, actually, there are no bad choices because when I make a bad choice, it's still good because I learn from it."

My mouth fell open and I looked at her quizzically. I had to ask her how she knew that—had she overheard one of the tapes I had been listening to or a conversation I'd had with another parent? Looking a little irritated at my ignorance, she sighed and stated, "I learned it by living it, Mom."

But the best endorsement I've ever heard for Love and Logic came a few weeks ago when Jenny told me, "Mom, I'm really glad you found Love and Logic." "Oh, really," I replied. "And why is that?" Jenny responded, "Because I remember what you used to be like."

DANETTE BRAUN

My son was asleep in the back seat and we had arrived at gymnastics. It was time to go in. Sometimes kids seem to be able to hear things in their sleep, so I asked him in a loud voice, "Do you want to walk in or should I carry you?" I was expecting a mumble or a nod at best—instead I got a still-asleep six-year-old saying in a slurred, sleepy voice, "If you carry me in…zzzz…are you going to charge me…zzzzzz?" and he continued sleeping. My wife and I broke out laughing. You know you've reached them when they give Love and Logic answers in their sleep.

RICK RADDATZ

My daughter, Royelle, knew about our plans for the day—to go to the Denver Zoo. The plan was for me to do Royelle's hair before we went. I kept calling and Royelle kept ignoring. I finally said, "It's time to go." Royelle appeared in a hat and said, "I can go like this." I told her that I needed to do her hair before we left, and now there was no time. I could see that we were not on track on this one.

I decided to use some of my new Love and Logic skills that I had learned in Stephanie Bryan's *Becoming a Love and Logic Parent* class. I left the house and went to ask my friend and neighbor Cecilia if she could keep Royelle for the day. Cecilia is a very nice person who always indulges the kids when they go to her house. I explained to her that she needed to be "Mabel, the baby-sitter from hell." The expectation for the day was that Cecilia would provide safe supervision without indulgence. That meant no cookies, no babying Royelle, no cartoons—only news. Cecilia reluctantly agreed.

When I came back to the house and told Royelle she would be staying with Cecilia for the day, she kicked, screamed, called me "stupid," and fought her way to Cecilia's. She said that she hated both of us and was not going to stay. Once I got her to Cecilia's, I left right away. Her brother, Marcus, and I went to the zoo and had a delightful time.

After the zoo, I picked Royelle up and took her home; I never said one word to her about what had happened. I did get a call from Cecilia reporting that Royelle had sat in the same spot the entire day; she also reported that she would never do that again—she just doesn't have what it takes to be a "Mabel."

As for Royelle, she must have learned a lesson that day because she has never done that again. And another great thing—Marcus also learned from Royelle's experience.

MARY FLOYD

This past weekend, I overheard my seven-year-old daughter, Caitlin, speaking with her four-year-old brother, Travis. Travis was whining and wanting to know why he could not play with her Barbie.

CAITLIN: Because I said no.

TRAVIS: I want to play with your Barbie!

CAITLIN: (calmly) I understand.

TRAVIS: You're mean!

CAITLIN: Probably so!

I had to laugh—maybe she's a Love and Logic teacher in training.

KELLY SMITH

As a parent, have you ever prepared a meal that one of your children didn't like? Followed by that child expressing their dislike? Well, this is how my family and I handled one suppertime. One of my sons, who is a very picky eater, was refusing to take little of what was being served this particular evening for supper. I noticed that and decided something had to be done about it during *that* meal.

It is a common practice for our family to have dessert at the end of a meal. I noticed that all of the other family members were getting enough to eat, so I made this enforceable statement: "I will not be serving dessert tonight."

Everyone continued to finish their meals without comment. However, this particular son stood up in protest, and ranted and raved: "I am going to eat ice cream! It is not fair that you serve bad meals so I'm hungry!"

Everyone ignored him and I said, "Bad decision." He continued to rant and rave that if I would make decent meals, he would get enough to eat and he wouldn't be hungry for ice cream.

I continued to say "bad decision" as he marched to the utility room, opened the freezer, and brought the ice cream to the kitchen. He continued to complain as he proceeded to open the ice cream bucket, pull out a scoop, and open the cupboard door for a bowl. I quietly said "bad decision" again and no family member said anything to feed into his anger!

Then, all of a sudden, he put the cover back on the ice cream and marched it back to the freezer as he continued to complain. He sat down and we ended our meal with prayers.

Later that night I went to teach a parenting class. One of the participants asked what I would have done if he had eaten that ice cream. I said I knew what I would *not* have done: wrestled it away from him. Upon more reflection I said I probably would have stopped by a store to buy enough treats for everyone but him and served them that night!

He never asked me what I would have done. He knew it would have been something bad because I had used those words before and he didn't like the outcome.

Isn't it great to get your point across without anger?

PEGGY IMHOLTE

My husband and I learned of Love and Logic through a friend several years ago and have embraced the philosophy in our parenting ever since. While our son is naturally a good-natured child, we believe the use of Love and Logic has enhanced his demeanor and has helped us to raise a responsible child. A number of our son's teachers have commented on how responsible he is. Our seven-year-old knows that when he is dealing with a problem of his own creation (e.g., forgotten homework or mis-placed library books), our response will be, "Oh, no! What are you going to do?" Now, before we can get the words out, he responds with, "I know. It's my responsibility."

My son and I were reading a story about a mouse named Oscar who insisted on dragging his blanket, Flannelle, everywhere he went even though he was getting too old. First, the parents tried unsuccessfully to rid their son of the blanket by saying that if he tucked it under his pillow before he went to sleep, the Blanket Fairy would replace it with a fabulous "big boy" present. But Oscar tucked his blanket under his pajamas instead, so of course the Blanket Fairy was unable to replace it. Next, the parents tried to dissuade their son from dragging the blanket around by using the "Vinegar Trick"—dipping his favorite corner of the blanket into vinegar. But again Oscar was able thwart his parents' plan by airing out the smell and choosing a different corner. Finally, when summer vacation was over, the parents simply said that Oscar could not take his blanket to school. I knew for sure that our son had learned to accept the consequences for his actions when he said, "Mama, why don't they just let him take the blanket to school? He'd be so embarrassed by the other kids, that he'd never do it again!"

THANKS FOR THE HELP,
RICK AND MICHELLE BLOOMFIELD

P.S. Unfortunately, the author of the mouse story must not be a Love and Logic parent, since in the story the parents solved Oscar's problem for him by cutting and sewing Oscar's blanket into a number of handkerchiefs so that Oscar could take Flannelle with him, wherever he went!

Here's how I came to be a Love and Logic parent. It was a long journey. My son was three. He was a terror. My style was explaining things to him—giving him a context by which he could make better decisions. That didn't work. His mother's approach was to give him commands—tell him what to do. That didn't work. Sometimes she would get so frustrated she would yell at him—and he would just laugh, giggle, or squeal with delight. We had no control. He whined all the time. It was parenting hell.

One day, he started to get a slight cough that grew worse and worse slowly throughout the day. By six o'clock in the evening, he was so hoarse that he couldn't even talk. He said with tears, "Daddy...I caan't taalk...I caan't taalk." He was the saddest little boy you ever saw. Some relatives were over and they were very concerned. When Mom went to call the doctor, my son asked in a slow, hoarse voice, "What will the doctor do?" I replied, "The doctor will look at your throat...and sometimes when you have throat problems, they will give you ice cream." My son's eyes lit up! He replied, "*Ice cream?!* Oh boy!" He said this in a full, strong voice, full of happiness and glee. We all just stared at him. I asked, "Does your throat really hurt? Or were you just fooling us?" He said, "Oh, I was just foolin'! Can I have some ice cream?"

My three-year-old son had been manipulating a whole house full of adults for an entire day with the skill of a professional actor. That was when I decided enough was enough for this kid. I started reading parenting books, and came across Love and Logic. I skipped right over the empathy part, and found the consequences section. I was elated. I started giving this kid some consequences. It was a lot better than before, but he was still such a sad little boy—honestly, truly sad. But at least he wasn't in control of the house.

Then my son outsmarted me again. He switched from *big* annoyances to *small* annoyances. So small, so subtle, that it was hard to give him a consequence for every one. And my consequences (mainly time-outs) felt too harsh to apply to every little affront—especially the way he screamed (etc.) when being taken from the room. Finally a therapist suggested a "1...2...3..." progressive counting approach to soften the consequences. Theoretically, it wasn't a warning—it was a progression towards a larger consequence. It worked *great* for one month. And in that month I at least knew what my son was capable of. That gave me hope. But after that month was over, it was hell again. My son had figured out that I was a three-count parent. My son had the freedom to do pretty much whatever he wanted—as long as he only did it twice.

It was then that I stumbled across the fact that there was more than one product in the Love and Logic series. I got hold of the *Four Steps to Responsibility* CD and actually heard Jim Fay speak. And that was the moment when it all came together for me as a parent. I was doing *everything* wrong. I got more Love and Logic books and I changed my technique overnight. I added empathy. I started saying, "No problem!" I stopped reminding. I offered fewer words, and took much more action. I stopped wishing for success. I started looking forward to failure! I "noticed" things he liked without commenting on them. We made up a chores sheet. I told the kids not to worry about picking up their toys in the living room—I'll clean them up! And I did—right into "storage," smiling the whole time. I have enough toys in storage right now to fund a month's worth of chores, and my son is the happiest he's ever been. My son's self-esteem is finally healthy. He asks how he can help around the house. He accepts consequences without a fight. He's honestly a joy to live with now, and I'm proud to take him anywhere. I never would have thought it possible just a few years ago. Love and Logic saved my son's life, and it changed mine forever.

RICK RADDATZ

Before taking the *Becoming a Love and Logic Parent* class from Stephanie Bryan, I used to scream, threaten, and punish my kids to get them out of the house in the morning. The biggest problem was getting them dressed. They would leave home for school crying, and I would leave angry and feeling bad.

After taking the class I was very skeptical about whether this would work so I decided to try an experiment. I went to a thrift store and bought really ugly clothes, one size too small, in my kids' least favorite colors, and with textures they did not like on their skin. I called them together and told them not to worry, that there would no longer be any yelling in the morning. I showed them the bags of "emergency clothes" I had purchased for them, hung the bags on their doors, and told them that if they weren't ready in the morning—no problem—they could just grab the bags and come on and get dressed on the way to school.

They looked in the bags at the clothes and said, "Yuck. That's stupid. We're not wearing that!" I didn't say a word; I just hung the bags on their doors.

That evening they put out their clothes for the next seven days. I told them they only needed to do it for the next morning or at the most for the next five days. They said they wanted to put them out for the next week. Guess they didn't want to take any chances. They continued to do this for the next year.

My kids are now ten and eleven and they are still laying their clothes out at night, sometimes for the next day, sometimes for the whole week. They never got to use their emergency bags of clothes. A couple of years later I returned the clothes, unworn, to the thrift store. On one level I'm very pleased that this worked, but on another level I'm a little disappointed; I really wanted them to have the experience of wearing those clothes.

MARY FLOYD

I use Love and Logic on campus and in my home. Naturally, I'm far more effective at work than at home. Typical of many families, mornings were a struggle with my eight-, six-, and four-year-old children all getting ready to fly in different directions. We've tried sticker charts, appealing to their desire to help, and of course the ever-ineffective screaming like a banshee about things that they really care nothing about, like Mom getting fired or something. Some techniques were effective for a while—others not.

A simple schedule change did the trick. Typically, I got them up and had them eating breakfast (ever so slowly of course) while I packed their lunches. It was easy to monitor and keep nudging them to chew faster while I was right there in the kitchen packing away! Needless to say…a minor change.

Now I set the timer and let them know that they'll probably be on schedule if they start getting dressed when the timer goes off. When I'm finished dressing, I usually have about twenty minutes left before I have to leave for work. If they are all dressed, with teeth brushed and at least the tangles combed out, I can easily finish hairstyles for my little girls *and* pack lunches. If not—not really a problem. School does serve a lunch and I don't mind paying for it since it saves me work in the mornings. Of course, my picky eaters aren't particularly pleased—and the thought of eating a school lunch is right up there with the dreaded withdrawal of Nintendo privileges. Voilà—they not only scramble to get ready promptly, but the added benefit of my four-year-old really needing an occasional bit of help has been recognized. If I have to help her, it takes away from the fifteen- to twenty-minute lunch-packing time, so big brother or sister pitches in to help!

ROBIN MACKE, PH.D.

My six-year-old son, Sean, wanted to write to tell you about how he solved a problem using the Love and Logic principles. His twin brother, Paul, had acted mean to the family dog, Coco. At our family meeting, Sean suggested as one of Paul's choices to have a "cuddle time" with Coco for a week. We let Paul decide how much time he wanted to play with her. He decided five minutes a day would be plenty. We had heard Barbara Colorosa talk about healing with the one you hurt and this sounded like a great idea. At first Paul did the bare minimum of "cuddling," but by the end of the week he had forgotten about the five minutes and actually seemed to be enjoying himself. We have had no problems with Paul or the dog since. We enjoy your ideas and have been attending your seminars, conferences, etc., whenever we can. It certainly seems to be paying off in all kinds of ways.

THANK YOU!
DEBBIE AND SEAN HARMON

Do you have a strong-willed child? A child who seems relentless in their endeavors? The strong-willed ones are good at that. Just when I thought that mine wasn't going to ever catch on, he did.

One Sunday as we parked the car to go into church, our son, John, asked if he could bring in a toy, a question he asked every week. My usual response was something like, "Church is not a place to play with toys. Feel free to play with the toy when we get home. In fact, we won't even stop anywhere unless we really have to so that you can get back to playing with the toy."

In keeping with his strong-willed nature, John would proceed to have a fit right there. At this time we would say something like, "Would you like to join us for church or go home to have some bedroom time?" He always opted to stay with us. Usually that meant a choice between sitting in the "quiet room" or with the rest of the congregation. Sometimes we sat in the quiet room. (I do not understand why they call it a "quiet" room, because not one child in there is quiet.)

One week, there must have been some divine intervention (or some quality time with one of my Love and Logic tapes), because when he asked me if he could bring the toy into church, this time I said, "Would you like to bring the toy into church and leave it in your pocket for the whole time we are there or would you like to leave it in the car?" I was prepared for the fit—after all I had gotten pretty good at it. Instead John said something pretty profound, "Mom, if you didn't give me so many choices, I wouldn't have to do so much thinking." I didn't know what to say. I wanted to laugh but instead managed, "Probably so."

The best part was, as we got out of the car, there was no fit. He doesn't ask to bring toys into church very often anymore. Oh, the wisdom!

JODI JACOBSON

My son Travis just started kindergarten and was in the hallway of his school when he heard a teacher talking to another student. This teacher ended her part of the conversation by saying, "Thanks for sharing!" Travis suddenly turned toward this teacher and said, "Hey! I know that! My mom says 'Thanks for sharing' all the time. She teaches that 'thanks for sharing' class. Mom has to use that stuff on my sister all the time but she *never* uses it on me!" This teacher called and told me the story and was quickly informed that Travis gets lots of Love and Logic at home too, just another phrase, "Probably so!" (ha)—thanks for sharing, Travis!

KELLY SMITH

My six-year-old son was walking through a restaurant all decorated for Halloween. Spiders, ghosts, and other cool things hung from the ceiling. He wasn't looking *at all* where he was going; instead he was looking at the decorations. Then it happened. He walked right into a table and knocked a plate off. He lunged to grab it, but he was too late and ended up sending the plate high in the air—flip—flip—flip—*crash!* The plate broke into a hundred pieces on the hard marble floor in an explosion that echoed through the restaurant far longer than it seems like it should have. My son managed to say, "Whoa, that was loud" in a clear, normal voice before the reality hit him, at which point he broke down completely and started to sob uncontrollably—mainly out of shock and perhaps embarrassment.

Instantly, "Helicopter" waitresses of all ages rushed to the scene saying things like, "Oh, it's all right! Don't worry! We'll pick it up! Don't cry! Don't cry! It's okay!" Luckily I got to him first and gave him a big hug and locked in the empathy without rescuing him by saying, "Pretty scary, huh?" He nodded and calmed down a bit.

But then to the shock of the waitresses nearby, I said to my son, "I'm afraid you are going to need to pay the waitress for that plate. Here's a dollar. You can pay me back when we get home." He walked over to a waitress and said, "Sorry I broke your plate," then handed her the dollar. The last thing she wanted to do was take a dollar from a clearly remorseful little boy, and she refused! I leaned over to the bartender and said, "Take the dollar, trust me, I'll explain later." I told my son to pay the bartender and he did. The waitresses were all giving me nasty, shocked looks.

A few minutes later, my son was over it. I sat down at the bar to tell my side of the story. All the waitresses gathered around with more mean nasty looks on their faces to hear what I had to say. I said, "I know it seemed like I was being cruel to have my son pay for the broken plate, but he broke it because he wasn't looking where he was going—and look how cool the end result is—nobody got angry. My son knows I love him. And he's going to do a few chores for me back at home to pay for that plate he broke and he'll probably feel great about it and feel great about himself—plus he may have actually learned something about watching where he's going." The bartender said, "Man—I never would have thought of turning it into a learning experience like that. That was really neat."

Half an hour later, we arrived at the shopping mall and entered through an expensive department store. My son walked down the exact center of the rather wide isle, and pointed out all the delicate glass Christmas ornaments he really liked and said things like, "I'm not touching that!" with a big smile on his face. Later that night he agreed to clean out a stinky garbage can for me and went off to bed saying, "I love you, Dad."

RICK RADDATZ

PART 3

Teens

The teen years can be very difficult. They can be a challenge for both the teen and the parents. The pressures and influences at this age are incredible and the choices our teens make can sometimes mean the difference between life and death.

Many parents are blessed to have teens that only push them a little—some have teens that push them to the limit. In both cases, Love and Logic has helped save the parents sanity and in some cases, the teen's life.

Many kids are lucky to have parents who started using Love and Logic when they were just a toddler—they have a real advantage: their teen years will go a little smoother. Some have parents who just discovered Love and Logic. These teens will hit a few more bumps in the road, but the good news is, it's not too late.

In the following stories you'll find both.

As little as six months ago, my thirteen-year-old son was on a path of trouble—not doing his schoolwork, not wanting to do anything around the house, hanging around the mall, trying to push the limits by skipping school. In short, he behaved like a "typical teenager." As a recently divorced single parent with no experience in this area, I had no idea how to handle the situation and actually was going about it in a confrontational and totally wrong manner.

A friend of mine, who had attended one of your classes in Denver, gave me your catalog. I started out with *Winning the Homework Battle* and found that it not only worked like a charm on my son's attitude, it also relieved me of the stress, and anxiety of dealing with it. With this under my belt, I next tried the principles outlined in *Love Me Enough to Set Some Limits* and again had incredible success. I recently completed the *Hormones and Wheels* series with similar good results. It's hard to believe that in a short six months my son's grades have improved to an acceptable level, he has started cleaning his room, and now he even makes his own bed without me ever having to ask him, does his own laundry, and regularly fixes his own meals. What a change for the better!

I must have listened to your tapes fifteen or twenty times and still listen to them every time I get in the car to run an errand or go on a trip. It helps me reinforce the Love and Logic principles and allows me to put them into practice a little bit more each time. For my son and I, they have done wonders, and when my parent friends complain about their teenagers' behavior, I hand them a catalog and mention the remarkable results your guidance has provided for my family.

PETE PENNINGA

A mother in my class explained that her son (fourteen) was ADD (so she had been deep into micro management!). After our Love and Logic class she decided to stop nagging him. So he never showered during the Easter school break (and she never nagged or reminded) and returned to school dirty, with his hair so greasy it clumped together, and spinach in his teeth—dressed in his new Easter clothing outfit.

The mother said she fully expected to hear from the school, especially because she taught at the elementary school just next door to the son's middle school. When she got home from school, she heard the shower running and couldn't imagine what was happening (sort of like the vacuum story—the mother didn't know what the sound was because it had been years since she had heard it from a distance!). She contained her amazement when her son came out clean and dressed. He said that his fourth-period teacher at school that day had come into the classroom and sniffed three times, then asked, "What is that smell?" The son said that he was afraid that the smell was him (which proves that he had some degree of under-standing!). Then he asked his mother, "Mom, do you think you could remind me to shower so I don't forget?" (her reminding before was called "nagging"). The mother, post–Love and Logic, was too smart to get hooked into owning his problem, so she said, "Oh honey, you remembered to shower today, you don't need me to remind you." Then (checkmate) her son's face lit up like a light bulb and he said, "Well, I'll just shower *every* day and that way I won't forget!"

The moral of the story is: the kids know! Nagging doesn't work! Bless the teacher for her part in catapulting a kid from zero to sixty with one simple question!

ABBIE VIANES

Though today I am a professional speaker and author, my formal education is in the world of accounting. I graduated from William Jewell College in Liberty, Missouri, in 1981 with an accounting degree and passed the CPA exam that fall. After working five years in public accounting and twenty years as a chief financial officer and chief executive officer in hospitals, I decided to change my career, but I have never quite lost the mentality of an accountant.

Accounts have a reputation of being stiff, dull, anal retentive, even boring! Come on, admit it! When you think of your accountant, you think of a person with the looks of Al Gore and the compulsive demeanor of Melvin Udall from the movie *As Good As It Gets*, don't you?

Case in point, two summers ago I was a keynote speaker for an educational conference in San Marcos, Texas. The speaker I followed liked people to get to know one another better during his programs by asking the audience questions from *The Little Book of Questions*. Those in attendance would raise a hand to answer in the affirmative.

He asked, "Have you ever passed gas and blamed it on someone else?" As a few brave souls sheepishly confessed, he told us about asking this question to a group of CPAs once and no one raised a hand. He believed they were telling the truth because it looked like none of them had passed gas in years. Following the program, one of the accountants approached him to state, "To make that logically possible, you would need three people. You would need one to pass gas, one to blame it on, and one to believe you." As the audience roared in laughter, I sat in my chair guilty of thinking the same logical thought. I guess fruit doesn't fall too far from the tree.

Even though accountants have a bad reputation for lacking in personality and creativity, we are not all as extreme as some like to believe. Some of us can even grasp and utilize the principles of Love and Logic.

I presented my educational collaboration program at a school in Wisconsin last February. I often include the principles of Love and Logic in a section where I encourage educators to be unafraid of failure.

During a break, the accounting teacher told me about a financial approach to using Love and Logic. He said he has a wonderful sixteen-year-old son who rarely caused him or his wife a moment's worth of trouble. The only chronic problem they experienced with the child was a lack of motivation in doing tasks he really didn't care to do. The most prevalent problem in this regard was with his homework.

The father said his son had been able to get A's and B's throughout school with little effort until his sophomore year, when he began to struggle with geometry and upper-level English. When the first nine-week report showed the poor marks in these subjects, the son received the standard discussion of the importance of grades. He buckled down for about three weeks, and then his work began to fall off as the holidays approached.

The semester report showed the son's grades had deteriorated from the first nine-week level, falling to D's. Having an analytical accountant's mind and knowing a bit about Love and Logic, the father began to develop his plan of action. He met with the teachers and found that the boy's grades were extreme to say the least. The son scored either 80–90 percent, or 20–30 percent. Armed with this information, he sat down with his son to discuss the situation.

The father carefully explained to the son that his decision to make poor grades may not have any immediate consequences, but poor grades could, and would, limit the colleges the son would be allowed to enter. In fact, the father said, if the son got C's and D's in high school, he would probably flunk out of college! He explained that without a college degree, the boy would be limited to a job paying $7–8 per hour. The accountant father calculated that earning $8 per hour would give the boy an annual gross earnings of $16,640. After calculating the income and social security taxes, he concluded the boy would net about $1,000 per month.

Upon hearing he would have a $1,000 a month in cash, the father said his son got a look on his face like, "Why am I working this hard if I will have that much money?"

At that point, the accountant outlined what it would cost the son to live out on his own. This included an apartment costing him $300 per month, food costing $250 per month, a junk car for $200 per month, plus another $150 in maintenance, gasoline, and insurance. The remaining $100 being spread out for utilities, phone, clothing, and medical expenses. The father told his son that he would basically make enough to survive, if that!

At this time, the father moved in for the kill. He told his son that upon careful consideration, the son's grades would not affect the standard of living for himself (the father) and his wife. The only standard of living affected by the son's poor grades would be that of the son. The father said, "Since you have decided to limit yourself to an $8 per hour standard of living, it would be wrong for us, as your parents who love you, to allow you to continue being accustomed to a higher standard of living than you will live on in the future. Since you chose this level, we don't want you to have such a shock in two years when you get out on your own!"

The boy seemed relieved he wasn't getting into trouble and seemed to believe he had gotten off lightly! That was until the night he asked to get a pizza! The father said, "Hey, that would be wonderful!" Then he got this very sad look on his face and said, "Oh I forgot, you are living on $1,000 per month and don't have the money for a pizza. I'm sorry." The lesson hit harder later that week when the son asked his father when they were going to the Packers game. The father said, "Man, I would like nothing more that to go to a Packers game with you, but you are living on $1,000 per month and don't have the cash to go." (The father told me he thought going on to the Packers game without his son would have reinforced the lesson, but he couldn't bring himself to go alone because it was always an activity they shared together.)

The son began to make the link between his grades and the standard of living he enjoyed on a daily basis. The father said the boy continued to have difficulty with responsibilities from time to time, but seemed to have been positively impacted by this circumstance. He also said his son responds more quickly to discussions about the seriousness of his responsibilities than in the past and with less input from his parents. Following up with the father, he was happy to report the son was making all A's in the first semester of his high school senior year.

KENT RADER

I can't begin to tell you what a dramatic and instant change my family has gone through for the past two weeks. My counselor lent me her Love and Logic *Hormones and Wheels* tapes. *Wow!*

I am a newly single mom with a fifteen-year-old daughter and a fourteen-year-old son. I am also a licensed foster parent for the state of Missouri and have many, many children in my care. I had the privilege of loving the last sibling group for five years before they were placed for adoption this summer. I sure wish I had had your tapes seven years ago when I started fostering.

These tapes have provided me with the greatest tools. Our lives will never be the same; I have always been a "tough love" mom. An iron hand in velvet glove mix that has worked fairly well for a number of years. However, since the children are getting older and *very hormonal* (especially my daughter, Kathryn), I needed new and improved tools. Love and Logic has done the trick. Kathryn has been my challenging child. After hearing your tapes and completely connecting on many levels, I couldn't wait to get home and watch the fireworks. I didn't have long to wait before Ms. Attitude walked through the doors and began her normal routine of harassing her brother and trying to manipulate me. Instead of being angry, I loved her with "I know" then "nice try" when she tried to get belligerent with me. My calm and cool reaction to her literally made her step back. She said, "Okay, what's the trick? What's up?" I replied, "I'm merely loving you and being supportive of you." She told me, "This isn't any fun, you won't argue with me!" I sweetly replied, "I know." She stomped from the room. My son was witness to this scene and literally rolled on the floor in laughter. I shared some Love and Logic techniques with him and he now uses them on his sister. After much protest and many attempts to shake the tree, she has for the most part stopped the major attitude. She knows her manipulative ways will no longer work, and that I will no longer hook into her anger and rebellion. It wasn't perfect overnight; I caught myself becoming angry on a couple of occasions and falling back into old patterns, but then I heard myself and I listened to what I was saying— and closed my mouth. She quickly picked up the pace and tried to further engage me, but this time to no avail.

I've used the delayed consequences, which is a wonderful tool. The kids hate it when I need time to gather my thoughts and think about what I should do about a problem. I had an opportunity to use your very example with a poor grade on my son, the honor student, who decided not to complete his work. He received a deficiency notice in English. I was very sad for him as I used (almost verbatim) the example on the *Hormones and Wheels* tape. It was wonderful when Andrew knocked on my bedroom door some thirty minutes later with a solution.

Jim, you're a genius. I'm ordering more programs from Love and Logic for my library and giving some as gifts. Your program has blessed my family so much in the short two weeks we've been working with it. I'm getting so many more hugs and kisses from my daughter and I'm a whole lot more huggable too. Thank you so much for sharing your wisdom.

ANGELA BIRDSONG

Dear Mr. Jim Fay,

I am an eighth-grade student and my parents are both teachers. They attended your conference this summer in Copper Mountain. I think your techniques of discipline are very interesting. I believe that my mom and dad enjoy the techniques. Although I think that your techniques are a lot better than some, I have to say, and please do not take this the wrong way, you have definitely created monsters in both of my parents.

All they seem to know is what you have taught them at your clinic. I do believe that it is working great for some of the students that they have to work with.

They are Jim Fay—all-the-way fans. I have to give you some credit, considering that Mom comes home after teaching summer school a lot happier now. So thank you.

SINCERELY,
ANNASTASIA M. MALCOLM

We have been using Love and Logic for about three weeks now. It has been great—no more yelling at our four daughters and no more lectures. We have had to bite our tongues many times, though.

My reason for writing this is to share what I overheard my oldest daughter tell her sister. She said, "I have been good for so long now, I think I forgot how to be bad." I felt both joy and sorrow as I heard this. Joy because I saw her self-esteem rise, and sorrow because I didn't realize that my "helpful" lectures and yelling made her feel like a bad kid.

I recommend Love and Logic books and tapes to all my friends struggling with parenting.

ANN MCCAULEY

I went to my son's basketball game the other night, and as I watched the referees, I noticed how they interacted with the players. They allowed them to play—didn't tell them what to do or how to do it, just observed and waited for them to make a mistake (probably secretly hoping that they made one!). When a foul occurred, the refs didn't yell and scream, lecture, threaten, or warn. They simply blew the whistle and issued the consequence! Can you imagine a basketball game where a foul occurs and the ref says, "Don't do that, it's not nice!" Then, "I told you not to do that! Now, you better stop it right now…or else!" And finally, "Okay! I've told you a million times already! If you foul one more time I'm going to give the other team a free-shot! And *I mean it!*"

What a joke that ref would be. Of course the game would be a total fiasco. Isn't it funny that parents on the sidelines get sooo mad at the refs too? They hate to see those logical consequences imposed on their "babies."

What a great lesson about the effectiveness of clear expectations (rules) and consistent, logical consequences.

BECCI CRAIG

Our son Jim liked to make choices, usually bad, and usually they hurt, so skipping school was very easy. One of his friends in the eighth grade already had achieved five felonies, so he could rely on that kid's experience to guide him to utter heights of freedom outside of school. Fortunately, Jim usually talked about what he was thinking, so I was a little prepared and I had four years of Love and Logic experience.

Jim's mentor taught him how to forge passes. In last-hour science class, Jim would merely state that he needed to go for special help to the resource room and the teacher became his unwitting accomplice. One less hormonal teenager out of class didn't hurt him any. Jim had a forged pass just in case he was challenged, which apparently didn't happen too often. In my opinion, middle schools should have no more than 200 students, instead of the 1,500 this one had. I can't blame the teachers, because at the end of the day they are at the least exhausted, if not brain dead.

Fortunately for Jim, his mother had come to get him for a dentist's appointment and arrived as Jim was happily walking around outside of the building with not a thought in his head about the appointment, or what would happen should he be caught in a freedom experience. Ruth called the office on her cell phone and inquired why Jim was running around outside. The secretary assured her that he was in science class. Ruth told the secretary to look out the window. Mother was correct! She called me and I put the plan into effect by merely rearranging my schedule.

When she and Jim got home, Jim came into my office and I asked him about what had happened. I told him that since he had made the choice to skip school, the consequence for his poor decision was that I would have to help him get to all his classes the next day. I mentioned that he needed to meet me in the foyer so I could start out the day with him. If he chose to not be there, I would have him paged over the PA system. When I arrived he had his nose pressed against the glass. Good choice! I walked with him to every class the next day, pulled up a chair, and sat right next to him. We had a wonderful day in class together. Father-and-son bonding is great.

I'm happy to report that Jim decided that going to school was his job and skipping was not in his best interest. He told me that he had to explain to quite a few students why his dad was in school with him. I believe that without Love and Logic training there would have been a parental explosion and other less desirable events.

ROBERT AND RUTH RIDDELL

It is my pleasure to host a third exchange student for the year. Each international student is a unique and richly rewarding experience that will last a lifetime. Elisabeth, my exchange daughter for this year, arrived in August expecting her exchange year to be nicely arranged and "done for her." This young lady at the age of seventeen years had never been required to do any household chores, help prepare meals, clean up after herself, etc. The extent of her pampered life dazzled me. In her home her father would wait for her to wake up and then drive her to school. It didn't appear to be a problem if she was late to school. I don't know if that is because her father is the assistant principal of the school or lateness isn't considered an issue in her situation. This bright, sweet, and sensitive young lady had no concerns upon arrival and no sense of responsibility for her stay.

Oh, fortunate teen, to come to my Love and Logic home! As you can imagine, she was in for a huge shock, as she quickly realized she would really be expected to make contributions to the family and manage herself. Her immediate reaction to these expectations was not a pretty sight.

The exchange program staff and her parents couldn't understand how she could be so miserable and like me so much. Oh, the power of *empathy!* Empathy rules! It was that empathy that confused them all and encouraged her to take ownership of her life.

The most difficult challenge for her was getting up on time for the school bus. She is an intelligent person and thought of many ways to put the responsibility for this task back on me. My response was the same. "Oh Elisabeth, that would be so sad if you missed the bus. How will you get to school?" The empathy and question did very much concern her. She continued to try to wiggle out of this responsibility by saying things like, "It's a special day tomorrow. Will you wake me just for tomorrow"? Or, "I don't know how to set the alarm." She had many more excuses. However, my response was always the same. I would give her a big loving smile and say, "Nice try."

The first couple of weeks were extremely difficult for her but I am delighted that she was motivated. I soon noticed that she was smiling more and actually "doing" for herself. One evening I walked by and overheard her phone conversation with her mother. "Mom, the hardest thing is to get up in the morning." I could only imagine the mother's concerned reply. My newly empowered daughter then defended the situation by replying, "But Mom, it's my responsibility to wake up." I was so happy for Elisabeth. Another indicator of her enormous progress was a conversation she was having with another exchange student. She was telling the student, "I could do nothing when I came here, now I can do some things!"

Her confidence soared. Gone were her anxieties about going to school, making friends, and her worries about having a successful year. I didn't realize how quickly and how meaningfully the Love and Logic philosophy would help Elisabeth. Our nation faced its greatest tragedy and my new daughter's family called to have her come back home. They made calls to her the entire week. It is my belief that it was her newfound confidence in herself that allowed Elisabeth to reassure her family that she can be safe, strong, and capable of handling any situation.

It was another reminder of how Love and Logic masterfully prepares our children to cope with the realities of the real world. If Elisabeth's stay in the U.S. ends today, she will take with her the most valuable lessons to serve her all her life.

BETH WEIR

I had a mother who had an ADD kid *and* husband! She is very much into managing and controlling. I invited her to take the Love and Logic class a second time (I tell them to bring their workbooks and just come—many have). The first time, it just sort of went over her head; the second time it stuck and this woman was ready for change.

One evening as she served dinner, her ADD son said something complimentary like, "Yuck, this dinner stinks. Can I have something else?" The mother remained calm and said that this was what they were having for dinner that evening. Well, he then demanded she take him to a fast food restaurant (what chutzpah!). She remained calm (again) and said that no, they were eating at home. So he upped the ante and began moaning how much he hated what they were having. His mother was empathetic and said that it must be so hard to be so hungry and not like what was served. She hoped he would like breakfast better. Well, he upped the ante to the point that she gave him a choice of staying at the table quietly or going into the next room to make that kind of noise. She held firm and off he went. In the next room he made paper airplanes on which he wrote "I'm *hungry*" and sailed them into the kitchen.

Well, he ended up not eating that evening and the next morning he came downstairs and threw himself on the family-room couch, saying that he was hungry and that his heart was beating fast (he was on Ritalin). So he ate a good breakfast. What a great lesson for him to learn to self-regulate and know what his body feels like without timely food to balance out the effects of the drug.

ABBIE VIANES

How grateful I am to have the Love and Logic philosophy in "my corner." How fortunate my daughter is to be able to learn about the world while she is still safely in my car. I've been using Love and Logic since our oldest, Christie, was four. Now seventeen, Christie has a cell phone that is in my name, but she is responsible for the cost. During spring break, we went to Georgia for a church mission trip and her boyfriend, James, stayed at our home to take care of the dogs, birds, and guinea pig.

Life is so traumatic at seventeen and Christie and James talked frequently. To the tune of $315.00. After deciding that pinching her head off was not a good plan, I showed her the bill and in my best Love and Logic voice asked her how she would like to handle it. Then I walked away. I could hear her and James talking as I left, examining the bill and trying to figure out how it could be so large. A few minutes later they came to me and said that they didn't think all the calls were actually theirs.

Being a good consultant I asked if they wanted me to help. They asked if I would call the company and see if the calls were really theirs. Since the bill is in my name (the phone is an old one that I got while I was a realtor and if I change it, I lose the great plan), I said I would do that, as I knew the representative would only deal with me.

When I called, the representative checked out the calls the kids had disputed and took them off. I went back to them with the good news—with a smile I reported that they were able to reduce the bill by $12.84. They couldn't believe it, but not once did Christie even imply that she wouldn't pay the bill. Then she told me that the reason the bill was so high was that she had thought that if the phone said "roaming" it would accrue roaming charges. So she had been very careful to only use it when it didn't say "roaming." She didn't know that her plan didn't have nationwide service.

I asked if she wanted me to call one more time and plead "super stupid" to see if it would help. I was pretty sure that that wouldn't do any good, but hey, consultants are willing to go the extra mile for their clients—even when they think it won't do any good. I found out that there was a special deal for "super stupid" people, and by the sound of things there a quite a few of them. We were able to get a onetime-only change to the plan that included nationwide long distance and no roaming and could be retroactive to before the trip to Georgia. It only would cost $59.99 per month instead of Christie's $29.99 plan that had turned into $315.00. Part of the plan requires that you have to keep it for at least two months. When I told her that she would owe $120.00 over the next two months, she hugged me and told me that I was the most wonderful mom in the universe.

Now that is Love and Logic! She thinks I'm wonderful and she's paying the bill. Isn't that great!

CHARI HICKS

While separating the laundry one afternoon, Mom notices two pair of her daughter's pants in the laundry basket. They are still folded. Mom also finds several pairs of her daughter's socks in the laundry basket, also still folded together. Her daughter had thrown these clean clothes back into the laundry basket instead of putting them away. Mom bought a new laundry basket for her daughter. She placed the discovered clean clothes, the dirty clothes, and the new laundry basket in her daughter's room.

DAUGHTER: (comes home and notices the clothes and basket) Why didn't you wash my clothes?

MOM: I am sorry honey, but from now on you will need to wash your own clothes, because I don't have time to rewash and refold your clean clothes. I will need the washer and dryer Monday, Wednesday, and Friday. Do you want to use the washer and dryer Tuesday, or Thursday?

About one month later:

MOM: (notices the new laundry basket is broken) Honey, we're going to the store to replace the broken laundry basket. I'd like you to come along and choose the one you want to buy.

DAUGHTER: *What?!* I'm not buying a new laundry basket!

MOM: No problem, I'll go and choose for you. I hope I don't spend more money than you were expecting to pay. Do you want the expense to come out of your savings account or your allowance?

DAUGHTER: That's not fair!

MOM: I know. Do you want the expense to come out of your savings account or your allowance?

DAUGHTER: I'm coming with you. And don't worry, I'm bringing my wallet.

Thank you, Love and Logic, for helping me teach my daughter to become a responsible young lady!

ANN MCCAULEY

I have a dear friend whose son was diagnosed with cardiomyopathy ("lazy heart") last summer. He was an exceptional athlete even at the freshman level, practicing with the varsity teams in multiple sports. He was very committed and always lived up to the challenge. For a child of his incredible talent and ability the diagnosis was surprising and especially devastating. It would mean no more cardio or contact sports at the least. At the best it meant an entirely new lifestyle and a need for a new faith in medical science along with the always steady faith in God in order to live out a "normal life span" with all the expectations and dreams it holds.

For a fifteen-year-old it was the end of his life. For his mother it was only the second beginning. The medical forecasts are frightening and the challenges for encouraging your child are amazing. She stepped up in every area, keeping herself updated on the newest developments in medical science, even bringing a new protocol to the attention of the leading doctor on her son's case. In the meantime she encouraged her son in golf, a sport he was allowed to play, and continued to encourage him in becoming involved in the sports he missed and loved in different ways.

Recently another friend shared her admiration for the mother's strength and told her how sorry she was for her, knowing how she had to live with the fact that she could lose her son at any minute. The mother's answer was based on a Love and Logic moment, when Charles Fay lost five friends over a cliff in one night. A night he made a great choice. My friend, a Love and Logic junkie, had the ultimate answer. She stated that *she* was the lucky one. She got to enjoy and celebrate her son every day, and her joy in watching every move, including mistakes (to be celebrated), was a gift; she felt sorry for the woman who expressed her sorrow. For she enjoyed and reveled in her son and daughter each day as if there was no tomorrow while the other assumed that she had years.

My friend has many challenges, but Love and Logic has been a mainstay in her life, providing inspiration, humor, understanding, and a way of loving and supporting her two wonderful children with all her heart.

CHRISTINE ISELIN

My son, a senior in high school, loved to come home for lunch with two of his friends. During lunchtime they were cussing, gossiping, and griping about everything in their lives. After listening to the *Hormones and Wheels* tape, I planned a significant learning experience and shared it with my son during one of our brief, fleeting happy moments together.

I told him that I was willing for them to come home and eat my special burritos as long as I was happy. But each day that I heard cussing and griping I would be unhappy and they were welcome to eat anywhere they chose except our house.

Well, the next day I heard my son say (as he and his friends walked by the open kitchen window), "Guys, we have to keep my mom happy or we won't be able to come here for lunch." They replied, "What are you talking about?" He explained the situation and thanks to Love and Logic I was able to enjoy their company at lunch until they graduated. The decision was up to them and relieved me of nagging and griping.

This experience also increased the respect in our relationship and we were all happier. My son is now the father of my two sweet grandchildren. I believe that the principles taught in Love and Logic made a great contribution toward the wonderful relationship I now have with my grown boy. My only regret is that I didn't learn about Love and Logic when he was very young.

DORIS E. THOMPSON

Once when I was doing a youth and parent workshop at a friend's church, an adolescent boy was giving the other youth teacher a serious run for her money and sanity with his misbehavior. He had disrupted the class and defied the teacher. When I came in to do my workshop with the same class, as he almost pulled the Venetian blind off the window, he looked at me defiantly and said, "I'm ADD you know." So I looked him in the eye and said, "Oh, you mean **A**in't **D**oing what you're supposed to be **D**oing?" I wasn't going to give him that crutch. I told him he was welcome to stay or go and that I would know he had chosen to go by the noise he made with his chair (he had been really grating it and bumping it). Well, I started the class, and I heard a little "screek" of his chair, so I looked at him and he looked at me testingly. So I allowed him that one and let him know by a wink and smile and continued on teaching. He stayed and never made another peep.

ABBIE VIANES

I am grateful for the opportunity to share the positive change that has occurred within my family since I learned about Love and Logic. In the fall of 1998 our family moved from the Midwest to Evergreen, Colorado. My husband was commuting weekly. The Evergreen Middle School PTA was sponsoring a presentation by Dr. Foster Cline about parenting adolescents using the principles of Love and Logic. Because I had to go to the airport anyway, I decided to stop at the school for the presentation. The last of our three children was beginning his first year of middle school. His sister was beginning her junior year at the high school. Neither of them was especially happy with our recent move. My husband and I were parenting in a disconnected fashion due to our separate living arrangements, even though that was temporary.

Our daughter had somehow been allowed to rule the home. We did not understand her behavior. We had until this recent move had a very stable and predictable lifestyle. We lived in an upper-middle-class neighborhood with strong family values within the home and community. She was volatile. She would warn us, "Don't make me mad!" I was afraid of her. I could not overpower her, even though I had tried on many occasions. We were at a loss for what to do. We were hoping that the move would give us all a fresh start.

That night at the school, Foster began to talk about allowing children to fail. Allow them the choice to make decisions, even if the consequences were difficult. I began to see that we had been rescuing our daughter from all the negative consequences of her behaviors. This was a strategy that I could suddenly understand, it was logical. It was about the message we give our children. When we rescue them, we are telling them we do not trust that they are capable of making decisions for themselves. I had, up until that point, thought I was being a caring parent. I suddenly realized that I had been more concerned about how I appeared to others, than about how my daughter learned to handle choices and consequences in her life. I was ashamed, but renewed and excited to begin to hand the responsibility back to her, where it had belonged all along. What a relief it was for me to say, "Wow, that's too bad, what are you going to do about that?" Yes! freedom from her grip, finally!

Those simple strategies transformed our lives. The message I am sure she began to receive from me was, "I know you can handle this." It empowered her to become assertive rather than aggressive. She still tried to arouse my emotions, but with this new strategy and the relief I was experiencing, I was fueled to maintain control and keep handing the situation back to her. I am forever grateful. Our family is now calm and unified. Our daughter can now trust us to handle all situations in a controlled manner. We feel like we are the parents. I feel strong and ever so grateful to that fall evening three years ago. Our daughter, who used to constantly threaten to move out, is now working toward rebuilding the relationship with us that had been put on hold while she was running the world. She is now free to continue growing up and away from us in a gradual and well-planned manner.

Since that time, as an early childhood special educator, I have shared the Love and Logic strategies and website with many parents, professional educators, in-service presentations, and the students at Red Rocks Community College, where I teach Early Childhood Professions 101.

Thank you for sharing this caring and effective way to be the best parents and educators that we can be.

GLORIA HADER, M.ED., ECSE

We have been a Love and Logic household for more than five years now. The first ten years without Love and Logic were extremely difficult. I can say beyond a doubt that Love and Logic has provided the backbone that has supported additional interventions as well as bringing joy to our home. I am a single parent who adopted a child of another race. This wonderful child has challenges including adoption issues, identity issues, attachment difficulties, and attention deficit disorder.

It takes a lot of energy to keep pace with my daughter. Love and Logic has allowed me to put the energy I use for discipline to a creative and fun approach. Stephanie is fifteen years old now and it still is delightful to apply the Love and Logic principles in new ways. I'd like to share one of my favorite stories, which still makes me chuckle.

My daughter does not enjoy chores. Since Love and Logic has become a way of life, chores have taken on a new importance around here. A daily chore for Stephanie is to put the rinsed dinner dishes into the dishwasher. I will run the dishwasher and she puts the dishes away. Stephanie preferred to bypass the washing part entirely and put the dishes, etc., directly back into the drawers and cabinets. This method of "doing the dishes" had been a problem for years and I had tried many different methods of dealing with it.

One Saturday morning I went downstairs to make breakfast. I reached for the frying pan and it was covered with whatever I had cooked previously. Today was a new day and a time for a new plan. I proceeded to prepare "breakfast in bed" for my sleeping child. The menu featured this morning was her absolute favorite—grilled cornbread with honey butter—plus my favorite—a side helping of natural consequences.

Stephanie was thrilled to be treated to her favorite breakfast in bed. I stayed and provided pleasant company while I watched her enjoy her food. When she was almost finished with her cornbread I worked it into the conversation just how easy it was to prepare this morning because I really didn't have to add much butter to cook it. There was enough grease in the pan already when I pulled it out of the cabinet. A look of horror and disgust rapidly appeared on her face. Fairly soon her face appeared confused. I have come to recognize this as a good sign. It was also apparent that she lost her appetite about then. I continued with my happy chat and took her breakfast tray back to the kitchen. Nothing more was ever said but the dishes are much cleaner in our house and have been ever since. I never ate a bite of breakfast that morning but I guarantee you it was delicious!

BETH WEIR

I am the parent of four busy children aged fifteen, fourteen, twelve, and twelve. Our twelve-year-old sixth-grader, Daniel, has honed the fine art of occasionally disrupting the classroom with outrageous behavior. Several months ago he stunned the staff and students of our Catholic school with his gutsy behavior of typing in "playboy.com" on the school computer during class. He never pushed enter and went to the site, but he earned the attention of every kid in the whole school, all of whom went home to discuss it with their parents and mentioned it to him 100 times at school. He was just given a warning by the principal. Three weeks ago he decided to test again by typing in "whitehouse.com." This time he made it onto the site and showed all the other kids before the classroom supervisor was able to stop him. He was sent to the office but managed to wiggle out of any punishment with a big story about how he really wanted to find a White House site. I had heard him discuss that site with his other siblings weeks before, so I knew he had done it on purpose. He did admit to me later that he knew it was a porn site before he typed it in. He was ecstatic about how the school could not do anything to him about it! I decided that delayed consequences was the method to use here and told him not to worry about it, I would get back to him on what would happen.

Three weeks later, Daniel came up to me and in the nicest way asked if he could use the upstairs computer to play games. (He does not know this computer does not even have access to the Internet.) I thought for a long time and then said with a big smile, "That will be fine, but I will have to supervise you when you use the computer in case you *accidentally* type in the name of a bad site—like what happened at school." Big silence, then he goes nuts. "What? That's not fair! I won't do that again! If you have to use the computer with me, I'll never get to play! You let Tom use it!" I calmly said, "Oh, he is not a problem in that area. I'll be happy to supervise you when I get time.

BaBye!" Big smile here, batting my eyes with love and affection, then turning away. It was a Jim Fay moment! I had to wait three weeks for this one!

JANE WHITE

I recently had a situation with my nineteen-year-old son, Scott, that I would like to share. (Wish I'd known about Love and Logic when he was younger— I sure would have done a lot of things differently. But I'm learning it's not too late. This stuff works with "adults" too!) We've had major battles with Scott taking dishes and glasses into his room and not returning them to the kitchen—sometimes there were leftover bits of food on them and chocolate milk, which dries in the bottom of glasses. We've made him wash the stuck-on stuff off by asking nicely, asking not so nicely, telling him, demanding, threatening, etc. This is a big issue with my husband, Scott's stepfather.

Scott also has a fish aquarium in his room. Last week he set a bowl of water on the counter to come to room temperature—after several days I suggested to him the temperature was probably okay and asked him to get it off the counter. He did—and took it to his room. Meanwhile, I had bought some grapes, which I wanted to put in the bowl, and I hadn't seen my bowl come back. He had been over at his friend's house for a couple days (spring break, plus he didn't have to work). I went into his room looking for my bowl—found it, but I also saw plates with leftover food and numerous glasses.

Now just the day before I'd listened to your tape *Didn't I Tell You to Take Out the Trash?* I liked the story about the mom who came home to a driveway of toys and how she got her kids up to take care of it. That story gave me a fun idea. I called my son at his friend's house. He was in quite a jovial mood. I used Jim Fay's "lilt" as I talked to him. "Scott, I just got my bowl out of your room and saw the most amazing thing!" With perked interest, he asked, "Really? What?" With joyful excitement, as if I'd found something awesomely wonderful, I described what I saw: "Oh, Scott, I saw plates—with food still on them! And glasses with dried-on chocolate milk! It was the most amazing thing to see!" A moment of silence. Scott's response, "Oh." Still quite joyful, I asked, "Scott, do you think you could do something about it by tonight?" He said yes and that he was going to come home tonight anyway. I said, "Good, look forward to seeing you!"

It's about a forty-minute drive from his friend's house to ours. Scott was home in less than an hour. He must have left pretty quickly after our conversation—and that's a first! He came in, didn't even take his coat off, and began hauling dishes and glasses to the kitchen. My husband watched in amazement, and asked what was going on as Scott went from his room to the kitchen with several loads. I verbalized what he was seeing: "Taking his dishes to the kitchen. Notice he still has his coat on?" My husband stood in puzzled amazement. I winked at him and quietly said, "Love and Logic."

KAREN KUBIAK

I always looked forward to my oldest daughter becoming a teenager. I dreamed of being the mother I never had as a sixteen-year-old who desperately needed to be understood. I envisioned four years of high school Kodak moments that we could share and savor. Having been a "troubled teenager" myself, I believed I possessed special gifts with adolescents. I studied parenting. I knew about offering choices, setting limits, and the importance of consistency. As a psychotherapist, I thought I was ready to stand tall in the face of adolescence. Instead, I was humbled and brought to my knees.

When my daughter, Ann, became a high school freshman, all hell broke loose. If there was a risk we hadn't thought of, she took it. We've been shocked and scared. Now we're preparing for her senior year in hopes that the worst is behind us. She's not addicted to drugs and didn't drop out of school. She's not dead, and she's looking forward to pulling her life together. Even as I write those words, I'm afraid the turnaround won't happen.

This story sounds dramatic. It is. The worst occurred her sophomore year. After struggling through months of relentless depression, Ann was prescribed Ritalin and antidepressants. Just as the medication was taking effect, one of her classmates hanged himself. Shortly thereafter, another classmate in her Catholic school hanged herself. My daughter, fraught with depression, grief, and anxiety, was hospitalized. The medications, combined with the trauma, had precipitated a manic episode we had not anticipated. She stayed in the hospital for several days, and was more profoundly depressed *and* angry than she had been when she entered. The doctor added sleeping medication. I worried she would overdose.

Formerly a conscientious, above-average student, Ann lost all interest in school. Her grades plummeted. She barely finished the year. When she'd threaten to quit school, all I could say while trying to stay calm was, "That's an option…but I don't think it's your best one." Somehow I kept my head, encouraged her to believe in herself, and tried to rebuild my confidence as her mother. I was very scared. I prayed for her survival and my sanity.

Several months after her hospitalization, we moved from North Carolina to Colorado for my husband's new job. We thought returning to Colorado would be a fresh start for our family, and give Ann an opportunity to make healthy friends. But change was slow to come. Her depression did not abate. Finally, after several antidepressants, an adolescent psychiatrist suggested she might be bipolar and benefit from a mood stabilizer. Bingo. The depression started to lift, but she would still refuse to get out of bed and go to school. Then just when I thought all was calm and she was back in school, another out-of-control episode would occur. This is the nature of bipolar depression. It also seems to be the nature of a turbulent, angry adolescence. Now her depression seems under control, but the mania still stymies us.

My sister-in-law, Kelly, lives here in Denver. She has been a great deal of support as we struggle through one crazy episode after another. She has empathized, and reminded us, that we are good parents. She recommended that I read *Parenting Teens with Love and Logic*. She read it several years ago when her oldest daughter flunked out of college, and also when her daughter would call for money. "Wow, that's too bad. What are you going to do about it?" she'd ask my befuddled niece. She had learned to empathize, and put the basketball back in her daughter's court. The results were amazing using one-liners and natural consequences.

I had read one of Fay and Cline's book, ten years ago, and knew the theory behind the work. But their tips seemed too gimmicky and complicated. I wanted to be genuine, authentic, and sincere. Now, realizing my approach wasn't all that effective, I tried the canned one-liners. I believe there's something behind the adage "A book comes into your hands when you most need it." I read the book earlier this month to help me better handle my eleven-year-old son's occasional opposition. I found the book's one-liners so effective with him that I continued to read on. I also absorbed one-liners off www.loveandlogic.com.

It was fortuitous that the website and the book were available when Ann bolted out the front door. She ran away last week with a car, a cell phone, and baby-sitting money. We didn't see her for two days. It was an event she had threatened, but this time she was prepared: she had the means to achieve her goal. After she left that night I was so exhausted from the months of trying to rein her in and protect her that I just went to bed and put her in God's hands. I knew there was no way to control her, and that underneath it all she had good judgment and the ability to keep herself safe. She also had friends with better judgment than hers.

I knew I had tried everything I could as a parent to help her. Though I was calm and nonreactive, I was beginning to feel fatalistic and hopeless. I slept with the Love and Logic book in my bed. Though I felt defeated, our family ran smoothly while she was gone. I didn't overreact to the situation. Instead, I called my sister-in-law and we brainstormed Love and Logic ideas that might help us find a way to manage the situation. Meanwhile, my husband angrily stormed out the door determined to find his firstborn princess.

Able to speak the language of Love and Logic, we thought through our options. We created a plan that kept us all calm and prepared to deal with the crisis. When we were able to leave a message with her on her cell phone, we told her that we loved her, empathized with her situation, and then asked her to come home and talk about her problems with us. If she didn't want to do that, could she please return the car? I worried that if we overreacted, we would push her into a corner and she would act on her anger. I feared a *Thelma and Louise* ending.

Miraculously, my husband calmed down. Using my "new brain," I didn't yell or threaten consequences, though my "old brain" was furious and fired up. Ann knew there would be consequences because of our consistency over the years. However, this time, according to the book, we used anticipatory consequences. So after she returned home, my husband and I took our sweet time figuring out the consequences. Meanwhile, the keys to her car remained safely wedged between my mattresses. Later that night, just like the book suggested, we continued with a barbecue for a family friend whose lovely daughter had just graduated with honors from a Catholic high school. (Imagine the irony of that!) My daughter came home that night, expecting to hash out our differences. I simply told her I was glad to have her home, but with the graduation party I unfortunately couldn't talk to her about it at that moment. "Let's talk about it later," I suggested. She looked dazed. What is this? Has Mom grown a brain or what?

Ann's teenage years have given me insight to our parenting styles. I, having been raised by permissive, inconsistent parents, vowed never to be a jellyfish. So I became more of a "Drill Sergeant." My husband, who grew up in an authoritarian, *Father Knows Best* family, is a man with a loud bark but no bite. He's a softy, and often a "Helicopter" parent. Sometimes, unbeknownst to either of us, we would "switch brains" and assume the parenting style of the other. Weird, huh? It's some consolation to me, after talking personally with Jim Fay, that he has never known two Drill Sergeants to marry, nor two Helicopters. I guess this is one of the mysteries of marriage. Now we're working on becoming "Consultants" to our teen. We're making suggestions, rather than telling her what to do. Of course, as always, there are limits and consequences. Now, more than ever, we believe the adage promoted in Love and Logic: "United we stand. Divided we fall."

The hardest part of our recent family crisis was coming to a mutual agreement about the consequences we would dole out. We took several days, and finally we were of one mind. Ann was baffled that we hadn't reacted in the way she had anticipated. What could be taking so long? What are they thinking? The waiting period gave us time to cool off, and gave her time to imagine the worst. As I had told my son earlier that week, "There'll be a consequence, but I don't want you to worry about it." And of course, he fretted about it until the final decision was in. All this, of course, was orchestrated out of lessons I read in the Love and Logic book. And now, when Ann is demanding an answer for a request that she expects to be granted, I simply reply: "I'll have to think about it and get back to you." Works like a charm.

Later, as Ann and I were able to talk about her situation, the conversation started to heat up and aspersions flew my way. I decided to use one of Fay's famous one-liners to cool things down: "This is the first time I've ever been a parent of a seventeen-year-old." She immediately calmed down and said, "And this is my first time to be a seventeen-year-old." Finally we were speaking the same language, using one-liners I could pull out quickly to deescalate a crisis: the language of Love and Logic. Next time she is able to talk with me again without attacking or yelling, I'm going to respond: "Thanks for sharing that." And then I'll shut up.

After I think about what has happened, I think about anger. How angry that boy was when he impulsively hanged himself. How angry, scared, and hopeless that girl might have felt when she killed herself. How devastated and empty their parents must feel. How angry I feel that their actions affected my daughter and our family, and how angry I have been that my daughter and our family have been traumatized. Maybe we've all been "drunk on anger," as Cline and Fay suggest. And maybe Ann has been acting out her anger, rather than talking about it.

Anger makes my blood boil. I feel the fire rise up in my chest. But then I think about the good advice proffered in the book: "Express sadness rather than anger." And then it all softens, and I feel empathy, sorrow, and the good fortune to have my daughter alive. As I read the book, I have renewed confidence in the future. Cline and Fay say that if the first eleven years of a child's life are good, then despite what happens in adolescence, life should turn for the better. I think the prognosis is good.

AUTHOR'S NAME WITHHELD BY REQUEST

My fifteen-year-old daughter, Stephanie, wanted to work at a camp for special needs children for the summer. She was thrilled when she got her call for the interview. After the call she handed me a small piece of paper with several cryptic sentences on it. "Here are the directions," she announced and bounced off toward her room. I asked, "Do you want to write these out fully and keep them or will you just remember them and keep them?" She bounced back, snatched them up, and said, "I'll rewrite them."

On the day of her interview I picked her up from school. As I pulled away from the parking space she tossed the very same piece of paper over my shoulder as I drove. "If these are your directions, do you want to explain them as I drive or do you want me to do my best to follow them?" "Follow them," she grunted. She settled back to read one of her favorite books. It has been Stephanie's habit for years to enter the car, read, and get out upon her arrival. My daughter is oblivious to everything in transit. She has never thought about "getting there."

I did indeed follow her directions to the best of my ability. As we were about to enter a different state, I informed her of our location. She said,

"Turn around." I asked her what she wanted to do next, but she was mute. I commented that we might need more direction, so I stopped at a repair shop. Stephanie darted out of the car but very soon returned with a smile and more verbal directions.

I followed the new directions until it became apparent that we needed yet another set of directions. "Oh, River Road, turn there!" she exclaimed. I turned and pulled over because it looked like the back end of an industrial park. Stephanie jumped out again and was back in a flash with more verbal directions. I hastened to follow her directions again and then I followed the next direction, which she herself made up as we drove.

After making circles around the countryside, I stopped and asked, "Now what are you going to do?" She tried desperately to make this my problem. I said, "Steph, you need to think. What are you going to do?" She was late for her interview, not happy, and is always prone to just act. She announced, "I'm getting out here because I think that building across that field and beyond that cyclone fence is the camp office." I pulled over and waited.

She was back in forty-five minutes and the following dialogue took place: "How did it go?" "I think I got the job!" "Great!" She talked happily about the camp, informing me that there are three nights of orientation before the actual beginning of camp. My thoughts were along the lines of, "Oh that's wonderful, we have several more opportunities for her to have some learning here." I knew I was definitely on the right track as we made our way home when she said, "Oh look! There's Riverview Road. Wasn't that on the directions?" My teen seemed to have gained new awareness of the details outside of the car. These details will certainly be necessary for both later directions and upcoming independent driving. Perhaps she's also learning that being "along for the ride" can be a much longer trip than "finding your own way."

BETH WEIR

Sooner or later you will be confronted with the time-honored tradition of skinny-dipping by boys. Our boys were certainly no exception! I came home from work and was met by my wife, who informed me that I had become a single parent. She said, "*Your* boys (implying that they certainly weren't hers) have been mooning traffic along the county road." This statement also implied that it was my fault for having the pond dug so close to the road. We live twenty-five miles from town, so traffic is not too frequent, but frequent enough to blow horns—and that is what attracted her attention.

Armed with my Love and Logic training, I took the back way to the pond. I couldn't remember reading any articles about such an occasion; however, the principles were there. I kept repeating, "Remember to treat them with respect, it's not too big a deal, it's not life-threatening, and whatever you do, don't crack up laughing." They heard me coming and I overheard them saying, "Pull up your suits, Dad's coming." When I finally came into their view, the three were innocently standing in a row with arms at their sides, looking like absolutely nothing had happened. They did look guilty as sin however. As calmly as possible I said, "How's the water?" "Fine" they replied. I thought I'd better get right to the point. "It's all right to go skinny-dipping. However, because some people might be offended at seeing your white bottoms, it would be better if you used the pond in the back of the house that is surrounded with brush." They all looked shocked that I didn't blow a fuse. Later they admitted that they really were mooning traffic. I thanked them for their honesty.

I told them that when I was a kid I had three years of skinny-dipping experience. At the time, when a unit on swimming was taught in the Duluth public schools (it was not co-ed), the boys did *not* wear suits. I had hoped to take the shock value out of my boys' experience and it really worked. I had help from another source; in Minnesota, when we are not petrified and frozen, we have the most ferocious, bloodthirsty mosquitoes in our part of the nation. The back pond had a thriving colony. As I remember, the boys went skinny-dipping only three times. Those bugs had such a feed on parts they had never even imagined that the problem took care of itself.

I was so glad for all the articles that I had read. Love and Logic really works!

ROBERT RIDDELL

Big fans of Love and Logic for years, we have used different parts of it at different times. Some days my husband and I feel like successful parents, some days that feeling is less evident. We have two daughters, sixteen and nine. They are both wonderful children, but I will discuss the teenager. She is an extremely bright, ambitious, and beautiful young lady. She is also extremely self-confident and self-directed.

We have a cabin in the mountains about one and a half hours from our house. We had planned to go for a long weekend, but she wanted to stay at home. I arranged for her to spend the first night with her grandparents, and the second night she could stay at home with phone-call checks. We thought we had an intelligent, well-thought-out plan.

The first night was fine of course. The second night I went to call her at 9 P.M. to make sure she was at home, and she answered the cell phone, saying she was on her way into the driveway. At about 10 P.M. I decided to do a check and she didn't answer the phone. I had the neighbor drive to our house to see if she was in the barn, which she wasn't. I continued to call until 11 P.M., then went to bed to a sleepless night.

At 6:30 A.M. I called her, with still no response. At this point I second-guessed every decision I had made, was sure she was dead in a ditch, etc. I called a friend, and asked her to drive out to see if she was at home, then called home again and she finally answered. First she made the mistake of lying, saying she had been home all night. I bluffed, saying that I had talked to someone who had seen her around town, then she confessed. Through it all, I remained calm and nonaccusing. At this point, I told her that we would discuss it when we got home, but try not to worry. She was appropriately contrite when we got home, and we told her we were still thinking of consequences, but not to worry. After a second sleepless night, we came up with the solution: *the truck-sitter!*

The next morning her father and I woke her up bright and early (more painful because she is not a morning person). She was more than welcome to drive the pickup, but since I couldn't stand to worry about where my truck was, she could feel free to use it when she had an approved truck-sitter. (Only the nine-year-old was a parent-approved truck-sitter.) She had to pay the truck-sitter, and respect the truck-sitter's bedtime. The truck-sitter would also accompany her in any other truck she wanted to ride in until we knew we no longer had to worry. She also had to apologize to all family members and neighbors she had inconvenienced during the weekend. The truck-sitter was more than thrilled to go to all of the exciting places, plus be paid for it. She also happens to be an extremely chatty child who reported all of those exciting events very innocently. This was a valuable lesson for all of us, and had a fairly happy ending.

RHONDA WILLINGHAM

I am a single father of two daughters, twelve and fourteen. Two years ago, I was close to resigning from parenting. My daughters were no longer blindly obeying my commands and I was caught up in the "super dad" syndrome. For years I had done it all, yard work, cooking, washing, cleaning, shopping, and mending. I had also started a business two years earlier that I ran from my home in addition to having a full-time job. I knew I couldn't continue like this. The saying "It's always darkest before the dawn" is so true. It just so happened the local middle school was offering something called Love and Logic. The timing couldn't have been better. They offered tapes to take home and listen to and I did. Over and over until I knew every story Jim and Foster told like an old nursery rhyme. I started changing my parenting style and was amazed at how quickly our relationships improved. We divided up the chores like the tape suggested. I could feel the sense of family developing. In October of 1999, I attended the instructor training in Denver, and came back and taught my first class in December.

Love and Logic has been exciting and fun, up until the day my twelve-year-old, Liz, missed her bus. I dropped my fourteen-year-old at her high school and headed for work. I had just arrived at work, and the call came in right before school was to start. The conversation went as follows:

LIZ: (sobbing loudly) Oh Daddy, I'm so sorry, I'm so sorry, ohhh!

DAD: Liz, what's the matter?

LIZ: I missed the bus, Daddy, I'm so sorry.

DAD: That's so sad. What are you going to do?

LIZ: Can't you come get me?

DAD: I'm so sorry honey, but I'm really busy here at work. What are you going to do?

LIZ: Could you call the school and tell them I won't be there?

DAD: What would I tell them the reason is for you staying home? I couldn't lie.

LIZ: What am I supposed to do, Dad?

DAD: I don't know, what are you going to do?

LIZ: (more sobbing)

DAD: Do you remember the plan we talked about last year if you missed the bus?

LIZ: I can't do that! (much more sobbing) How do I call a taxi?

DAD: You might try the yellow pages under "taxis." Honey, I really need to get back to work. Good luck.

Fortunately, we had formulated a contingency plan the year before; there would be money in my dresser, a taxi would be called, and the fare would be paid back out of her wages from the business. I fought the urge to rescue. My first call was to the school to let the principal know what was happening. The second call was to the cab company with the biggest ad in the yellow pages. After explaining the situation to the dispatcher, she told me my daughter had indeed called and a taxi was sent. I hung up and the tears came to my eyes and I understood that being a good parent isn't always fun.

The principal called to let me know she had arrived but was more than fifteen minutes late. He asked if the absence was excused or unexcused. I told him unexcused. He informed me she would have to sit in ISS (in-school suspension) for half a day. The next morning, as my older daughter and I were leaving the house, I went into Liz's room, gave her a kiss, and told her I loved her and to have a good day at school. No reminders!

Two weeks after the incident, I picked up Liz from her friend's house, where she had been watching movies. When she got into the car, she told me, in a dramatic fashion, she had just watched *The Bone Collector*. I asked her if it was a scary movie. She told me it was about a taxi driver who tortured his passengers. She then empathetically said, "Dad, I'm never going to miss the bus again!"

Thanks to Love and Logic, both of us grew up a little that day and I haven't had to worry about missed buses. Thanks Jim and Foster!

SCOTT HIGHLAND

My eighteen-year-old son had just graduated from high school and wanted to move into an apartment with a friend. They waited tables together and were ready to launch into the great adventure of living away from home, paying all their own bills, and being self-sufficient. "Mom, you've got to sign this *now,* because if you sign a lease by ten o'clock tomorrow morning, the first month's rent is half off!"

My heart was pounding. I could feel its beat throbbing in my neck and head, and there was a knot in the pit of my stomach. A major power struggle was brewing. My mind was racing for phrases, strategies, *anything* from the Love and Logic classes I teach, to defuse what could be a nasty argument. And then, I remembered I didn't have to know what to do immediately. All I had to do right then was say what *I would do.* Setting limits by letting my child know how I operate is completely enforceable.

I took a deep breath. "Brandon, I take my time when I make big decisions like this. I'll need to think about that and let you know in the morning." "But Mom! Just sign it now. I'm good for the money, I have a job, and you'll never have to pay for anything."

Another possible argument could follow if I said anything other than what I would do.

"Well, I'm sure that's true. But I take time to make big decisions like that. I'll let you know in the morning."

"*Mom!*" demanded Brandon, to which I asked, "When will I let you know?" He sighed and said, "In the morning. But I don't see why you can't just sign it. Don't you trust me?" This strong-willed child does not give up easily. "Love you," I said. "I'll let you know in the morning."

Before drifting off to sleep I thought of options I could give Brandon. Like a lightning bolt the thought came to me that I could operate like a bank. The next morning I would tell my son that I would be happy to co-sign the lease under one of two conditions: if he had good credit with me, or if he had collateral to back up one month's rent. I smiled to myself and slept soundly.

"So, Mom. Did you decide? Will you sign it?" "I'd be happy to sign it under either one of two conditions. I'm going to operate just like a bank operates. I'll sign if you have good credit with me…" "I don't have good credit with you." "Right. So that just leaves one other option. I'll sign if you give me collateral worth one month's rent." "What? That's $500! Where am I supposed to get that much money?" I was ready for this one. I just shrugged my shoulders and said, "Wow, I don't know. Good luck to you, though. If anyone can figure this out, I'm sure you can."

I went to work with a spring in my step and a song in my heart. The problem was residing within the skin of the person who owned it. I could almost smell the smoke of the wheels of my son's brain turning as he thought about ways to come up with the money.

An hour and a half later, my phone rang at work. Brandon said he would give me his paycheck and equipment he owned totaling $500 for collateral. When he did, I signed the lease and he moved into his apartment.

What followed was one of the most difficult times in my son's life. He discovered that his colleague at work was not trustworthy. Many days he laid out of work and let my son carry the total weight of the bills and rent. Brandon was working sixty hours a week and spending all his money just paying the bills; there was nothing left for entertainment.

Fortunately, the lease was only for six months and Brandon moved back home, much wiser than when he left. He decided college was definitely the place to be and is now in his second year. He has great aspirations to become a physical therapist, and I have no doubt that his memories of those difficult days will be a catalyst to help him overcome the tough times that come in college and in life.

SHARON RHODES HALL

My fifteen-year-old daughter's love is rowing. This sport requires her to participate as often as five or six days per week, two to three hours each practice. There are other things in her life that require her participation as well. Among these activities, she barely endures homework and absolutely loathes chores. These things are higher on my list of values than rowing.

It was Thursday night and I noticed her weekend chores were not completed as she had tried to make me believe. I said I'd be happy to take her rowing when she finished her chores from last week. I put myself in my room early that evening to avoid reminding her—or worse!

Friday morning came and she assured me her wash was near completion. I hadn't heard a washer or dryer for days. I went to the laundry area and dirty clothes were everywhere, as they had been for the past week. When I brought this to her attention, she had the beginnings of a large tantrum. I said, "Sorry you are so loud. I'm leaving now. You'll have to take the bus to school." I turned and left the house to avoid watching her tantrum escalate. No rowing today.

Friday evening she brought home her report card. It was a fabulous one for her—only one D as opposed to the previous four. I was happy for her because she was proud. She wanted to take her report card to show our dear friends. We spent the evening with them.

Saturday morning came and she was excited to go rowing. The clothes were still on the floor. "But Mom, I got a good report card." Her pleading and begging turned to anger rather quickly. I knew if I didn't hold fast to my limits I'd be at this place again very soon. I empathized and went for a walk so as to remove her audience for the tantrum.

I felt terrible. I wanted her to row. I enjoy having my child pursue her passion. My walking and talking partner, Bob, has been a longtime friend— long before Love and Logic entered our household. He has listened well.

I complained to him about how bad I felt to leave her behind this morning. He knows I want to be a terrific mom. He said, "Yes, Beth, she's not rowing this morning, she's *growing!*" At that moment I once again felt like and awesome Love and Logic mom!

BETH WEIR

Parents of a sixteen-year-old boy called me to say their son had just driven his car through the garage door. It was a Friday afternoon and they had been planning to go out to dinner by themselves that evening. I reminded them of the Love and Logic principle that parents take good care of themselves. We discussed that they could do the first two steps in the problem-solving model, go out to dinner, and continue the next day.

They arrived home, stayed calm, locked in the empathy, and then gave their son the power message: "What are you going to do about it." To their astonishment, he moved into "problem solving" and came up with a plan. He would clean up the mess, ask his boss for more hours of work that summer, and pay for the damage. The parents had wanted him to work more hours during the summer; he had been planning on working fewer hours and then hanging out with his friends. The parents put a claim in with their insurance company, used their son's money to pay the deductible, and put the balance into his college fund.

STEPHANIE BRYAN

PART 4

Educators

From the very first day we take our little ones to school, life changes— for them and for us. Every day that our children go off to school, we are putting their future in the hands of someone else. Teachers, principals, counselors, and the school staff are all of a sudden in charge of our child's day. How lucky we are when the teachers and staff use Love and Logic.

I'm sure we can all remember back to our childhood and the teachers we loved, and those we didn't. The ones who made you smile, and those who made you cringe. And what about the teachers? As they watch the kids walk into the class for the first time, they can recognize the ones who will make life easy, and those who will make their blood pressure soar.

Working with children can be incredibly rewarding, or incredibly stressful. Each day educators face the unexpected—sometimes from the students, sometimes from the parents. The challenges are incredible, yet as they teach, they also learn. They learn things that no one ever mentioned while they were in "teaching school." Had these things been mentioned, many people may have chosen a different field. Luckily, many schools are filled with those who want to be there and help make a difference for our kids, and our society. How lucky we are to have them.

In the following pages you will read stories from educators who chose to make working with children rewarding.

The other day I had the opportunity to use the steps to guiding children to own and solve their problems. We were in the middle of a spelling test when a student frantically rushed up to me and said, "My sentence won't fit on my paper!" I glanced over and noticed he had plenty of room on the next line, but instead of telling him what to do, I put a blank look on my face and replied, "Oh, what are you going to do?" He just looked at me for a few seconds and I could see the wheels turning in his brain! He hurried back to his desk and rummaged through it anxiously. Finding what he was looking for, he bounced up and asked for a piece of tape. I was a little nervous about what he was doing, but I gave him a piece and continued with the test.

When he turned his test in, I saw that he had ripped the corner off another piece of paper and taped it to the edge of his test. Now his sentence fit perfectly! Oh, the creativity of children's minds when they solve their own problems!

CHRISTY PRESTON

My teacher, Miss Eisenhardt, is really nice; she's a Love and Logic teacher. She lets us do our own work how we want it. We get to be in charge of things in our class and make decisions. I wish all teachers and parents knew Love and Logic.

SINCERELY,
HANNAH ANDERSON

P.S. When my mom says, "I love you too much to argue," it kind of annoys me, but it makes me feel good to know that she loves me.

He sauntered into the room with a demeanor that called out, "Attitude." His oversized shirt hung way down over his baggy pants. He slouched in, shuffling his feet. My new student. A snippet from his file stated tersely, "Do not touch this child." Some investigation revealed that the time spent in his previous school had included several less-than-positive interactions with school personnel. One goal I set was rather unusual. It had nothing to do with curriculum or academic achievement. He would be in my room for just a short time, since he arrived in late winter. My goal was to get him to "high five," as the other kids were doing.

I had started the daily greeting of eye contact, smile, and friendly touch (high five) at the beginning of the school year, and really liked the results. Nearly all of the fifth-graders would do it, and those who didn't put up a hand got just a light, one-fingered touch on the shoulder. I started to joke around with the kids, and wish them "Merry Christmas," "Happy Halloween," or whatever other holiday I could think of, no matter what day it was. They ate it up. At the end of each day, the class would wait with their hands out to be "high-fived" and excused with some other closing phrase. Why? At every Love and Logic workshop I have attended, we have been encouraged to use smile, eye contact, and friendly touch. This has become a classroom ritual, in combination with the sign by the clock, which says, "I will like you no matter how you do in this class." It is my hope that students *will* feel valued and liked. (The sign is posted by the clock to guarantee that it will be read by most students daily.)

This year, I asked my new students what they had heard about the class, and they replied, "We heard that you do a hand-slap." A few days ago, one of our teachers didn't make it to the outside door to greet her class. A student of hers was very alarmed and said, "Our teacher isn't at the door! There must be something wrong!" He was very relieved to find that she was in the room. So, add another benefit of the daily greeting—a sense of security for the kids.

And my resistant new student? Before too many days had passed, he was accepting my high five, with a tiny smile escaping from his lips. Did it make an impact on him? I think he left knowing there was a caring spirit in our class.

Jim Fay also encourages us to greet everyone we pass in the hall. Those cool sixth-graders, the oldest kids in our school, will usually not return a spoken greeting, but they will reciprocate with a small wave. In our world of diminishing face-to-face contact with other people, eye contact, smile, and friendly touch can make a difference. And they don't make a dent in the budget.

Carol Gwynn

Have you ever had a student that was just a bit too savvy and street-smart for his or her own good? You know, quick with a clever rejoinder, always ready to call your bluff, and charming enough to pull off the sassy behavior? Eight-year-old Evan was such a student for me. From the first day of second grade he was ready to challenge my authority and rabble-rouse at every opportunity. Unfortunately for poor Evan, I had attended the Love and Logic seminar in Wichita just a few weeks earlier, and I had a new attitude. Poor little guy!

Our school requires that students run laps during recess for minor behavioral infractions, the number of laps being at the teacher's discretion. (The logic being that if they have the energy to cause trouble, they should probably run it off at an appropriate time.) After my experience at the seminar, I decided that I would have the students assign themselves the number of laps they needed to help them remember correct behavior. It surprised me how well the students chose numbers of laps that really were appropriate to their behaviors. Then came Evan.

The day soon came when he was required to choose a number of laps to run at recess. "Well," he said with that look of calculation of his face. "Let's see…maybe four. No! Make it ten! How about twenty?" He eyed me, the wheels and cogs turning. I knew he was trying to manipulate me into giving him a break. "No! I think I should run one hundred laps!"

"Really?!" I asked. "You sure of that?" "Yeah! That'll do it!" He grinned and looked at the class. They were in an uproar. "Ahhh! She'll never make him!" "No way!" "She'll let him off the hook!"

"Okay," I said sadly. "Wow…you've made a hard decision…I bet your feet get tired." Evan stood there, stunned. You could have heard a pin drop, and the class went to work with sober resolve. I notified the principal and contacted his parents. The die was cast.

Starting the next recess, and for the entire week following, little Evan walked and ran laps at recess. Sometimes his friends would walk sympathetically with him. I helped him keep count. I let him sit for a few minutes. I let him get extra drinks. I hugged him a lot. "Boy, sweetie," I would say tenderly. "You must be tried of walking." Or, "Wow, big guy, I think you made a very difficult choice. Are you okay?"

Evan finally finished his laps, and I am happy to report that he had a great year in second grade. He treated me respectfully and with affection all year. And no one—not a single student—ever, ever, *ever* called my bluff. And here is the best thing. Evan hated to leave at the end of the year, and he asked if he could visit me his whole life. How about that?

KATHY BENNETT

Dear Charles,

I am a principal of a small elementary school in Ashland, Oregon. Last year I set aside money to send a group of eight or nine classified employees to a Love and Logic conference you gave last spring. The staff had been in turmoil and wanting more "punishments" and "rules."

Wow, you helped save our school and build a terrific foundation for us to re-create our philosophy and plan. The group came back empowered and in love with Love and Logic. They quoted you to me and insisted that we bring it to all the staff and parents.

Even though I have been a proponent of Love and Logic since I moved to Oregon in 1992, I didn't really know how to use it as a foundation for our interactions with children. This year I am lucky enough to have come to the administrator training and hope someday to be able to attend one in the summer.

Anyway, thank you for making the difference with my staff and sharing your enthusiasm and knowledge. We now have ongoing in-service and a strong lending library of Love and Logic materials. I know I cannot thank you enough for your terrific work helping all of us do a better job with children. You certainly lit the spark in my staff and turned the school into a more positive, productive, and growing learning community.

BARBARA FIELDS

103

A woman in one of my Love and Logic classes shared an experience with me that she had with her twelve-year-old son. Those who think it requires a great deal of experience to use these principles effectively might be interested to know that the author of this story had only been in class for four weeks when this incident occurred. She requested that she remain anonymous.

CHRIS HALL

One day while I was at work I received a call from the principal of my son's elementary school. He informed me that my son, Justin (not his real name), had been suspended from school for displaying lewd behavior on the playground. For a few moments I couldn't even speak as I tried to regain my composure. The principal went on to tell me that my son was with a group of boys who were all displaying this behavior and when an adult aide approached them and asked them to stop they ignored her. I asked him to describe what it was they were doing. He gave me a few details but added that for the most part it was too lewd to describe. I actually felt physically ill. I had been attending a Love and Logic class and as I tried to apply the principles I had been learning, I couldn't! I thought to myself, "This problem is much too serious for Love and Logic!"

I began to think of what I could do to punish him. I would ground him…for a very long time! I would tell him that he could no longer be trusted around his friends, so he would no longer be allowed to play with them. But none of it seemed to make any sense, so I picked up the phone and called the instructor from my Love and Logic class. As I described the situation to her, she made the comment that this experience must have been totally humiliating for Justin and that the natural consequences of his behavior had already begun. My job was to make sure I did not distract him from those consequences. She reminded me to give him lots of empathy and ask lots of questions, as questions tend to keep people in the thinking part of their brain instead of forcing them to fight or flight.

That night as I drove home I practiced the questions she had suggested I ask. I had actually written down the questions while I was still on the phone with her so that I wouldn't forget them, and also so I could rehearse them before I got home. I walked in the door to see a boy who was scared to death. He was visibly shaking. I didn't have to reach very far to find the empathy I was looking for. (I had purposely put off talking to Justin over the phone so that I could formulate a plan and be sure that my knee-jerk reaction of anger was over. I also had arranged for he and I to be home alone.)

I walked across the room to him, gave him a hug, and said, "Hey Justin, it sounds like you've had a rotten day." He sobbed as I hugged him. When he had calmed down I asked him, "Do you want to tell me what happened today?" He replied, "I don't know." I started to just gently ask him questions based on the things the principal had already told me. I asked him, "What time did it happen? Where did it happen? Who was there?" I finally got around to asking him if he would show me what they were doing, but he wouldn't. I said, "Justin, are you embarrassed to show me?" He shook his head yes and started to cry. I asked him, "Was everyone laughing while all of you were doing this?" He replied, "Yes." I said, "Do you think the other kids were laughing because they thought it was funny, or because they were embarrassed?" His reply was, "I think they were laughing because they were embarrassed." I asked him, "Where did you get this idea to imitate?" To his reply—"I don't know, Mom"—I asked, "A joke maybe, a movie, a song you heard?"

"No, Mom," he responded. "It was a show my friends saw about horses." "Were the horses in the show mating?" I asked. He shook his head yes. Well—there was the pearl I had been looking for. The principal had eluded that they had been imitating sexual behavior. Now I knew what had really happened. Had I come in yelling, screaming, and accusing...can you imagine? More importantly, he never would have told me what they were really doing.

"Can I ask you a question, Justin?" He nodded. "Was there ever a time while all of this was going on, that a little voice inside you was saying—'Justin stop! This doesn't feel right'?" He nodded yes and started to sob again. "Do you know why you chose not to listen?" I asked. "I guess I just listened to my friends instead," he replied. I asked him, "Are you happy with the way it turned out?" He shook his head emphatically and said, "No, Mom."

In the Love and Logic class, I had just learned about the *Five-Step Problem-Solving Process,* and I was ready for the big question. With all the love and empathy I could muster, I said, "Oh Justin, I feel so bad. What are you going to do?" He stared at me in amazement.

"What?" he answered with surprise. "Nothing...I mean I'm suspended, what can I do?" I was excited now. "Well you know," I began, "we have seven kids. This isn't the first time something like this has happened. Would you like to hear some ways I have seen some of the other kids handle it?" He was interested! I offered some ways he could put things right again—apologizing to the aide, apologizing to the principal, apologizing to his friends for not being a better example. Then I gave him a big hug and we ended the discussion.

My doubts about not using traditional punishment dissolved over the next few days. The rest of the boys all got grounded. It was a tough week for Justin, facing everyone the next day, making apologies. On the third day they counted the ballots for sixth-grade student council candidates. Justin won and he was called to the front of the room while everyone applauded. Then his teacher took him outside in the hall. She told him she was very sorry, but anyone who had been suspended could not hold the office of student council representative. My heart broke that night as he told me what happened and tearfully said, "Oh Mom, if only I could take it back." We were closer than ever. He had made a bad choice and had paid the price for it. He saw me as someone who had helped him through it.

Over the next few weeks, as I talked to the other parents, I came to realize that they had no idea what had really happened. Some of the boys had lied to their parents while others just got through their punishment. My son had learned a valuable and powerful lesson about self-respect.

As Jim Fay and David Funk have stated in the *Teaching with Love and Logic: Taking Control of the Classroom* audiocassettes, if we were doctors repeatedly prescribing the same medicine that did not cure the problem, we would be fired. But as disciplinarians, we continuously prescribe the same detention, over and over again, that doesn't work.

I have begun to apply Love and Logic to my students serving detention. When they earn detention with me, I ask them the type of high-level thinking questions that you have "prescribed" in Love and Logic. Here are some of my detention conference questions: "On a scale of 1 to 10, with

10 being the best and 1 being the worst, how would you rate your behavior in my classroom?" "How do you feel about that?" "Is this the best place for that behavior?" "Is the misbehavior really necessary?" "What do you think will happen if this behavior continues?" "What are some other things that might happen if the behavior continues?" "If there wasn't a rule against talking, being out of seat, not keeping hands to self, disrespect (etc.), you wouldn't be in trouble. Do you think we should get rid of the rule?" "Thanks for giving it some thought."

I document this conference and share it with the parents and administrators when it becomes necessary. During these conferences, I find that students are very aware that the behavior is not appropriate, and that they know the expectations and the consequences. So this allows me to precede on to other "prescriptions" in the future. I make it clear to the student during this conference that if the detention consequence is not working, we must find something else, and I will let the student know what that "something else" is when he or she chooses to earn the consequence.

Thank you, Love and Logic, for helping me talk to students by getting them into the thinking state, because this allows the students reflect on their behavior choices.

CHERYL FRANKLIN

I am an elementary school principal in Vancouver, Washington. Many of our staff members have embraced Love and Logic principles and are having success in their classrooms with student behaviors. This is due to a Love and Logic study group at our school led by our school counselor, the Jim Fay and Charles Fay workshops we have attended, and the Love and Logic books and tapes we have recently purchased.

I have also experienced success dealing with student's behavior. Specifically, I recently suspended a couple of students for fighting. I tried to show empathy when I told them what their consequences were, and the students left my office to go home literally apologizing for their behavior and thanking me for allowing them to be suspended for only two days. It went something like this:

PRINCIPAL: I am so sorry you both chose to fight and created this problem for yourselves. Unfortunately, what happens when students fight at our school?

STUDENTS: They get suspended?

PRINCIPAL: Right. I would be willing to work with both of you now, however. In fact, I will let you decide how many days you will be suspended. We would need to do at least two or three days. What do you think?

STUDENTS: Two days sounds good.

PRINCIPAL: Okay, I would agree to that. I have really good news for you both (all the while, I have a big smile on my face). I would be willing to conference with you and your parents three days from now and if you really want to come back to school and feel that you can act responsibly, I will let you come back with a clean slate!

STUDENTS: Really? Thank you, Mr. Homnick.

This approach works well. Students cannot blame me for their suspension since this is the school's policy and is a result of choices they made. Ultimately, they will take responsibility for their choices and make a plan to improve their behavior before they are allowed to return to class. If their parents do not support the consequence, I simply show them our school's student management handbook and point out where it says that students can be suspended for fighting at our school. For the parents who want to focus on the fact that their child did not start the fight and therefore should not be suspended, I simply point to the paragraph where it says that it is the responsibility of the student who did not initiate the fight to deal with the situation in a nonviolent manner, and several other choices are listed.

CRAIG HOMNICK

I am a first- and second-grade teacher of a multiage classroom in Spokane, Washington. I had a little boy in my class who was unmotivated and very quiet. I found out from his father that he hated school and preferred to be home playing soccer or sports. He refused to write for me unless I gave him individual time, which extended past the class period. I was able to attend Jim Fay's administrators conference in Las Vegas. When I returned I decided to try the observation technique Jim talked about on this student. I would comment to the boy two or more observations. He gradually started smiling and talking to me. I continued until the end of the school year. I observed his drawings, his glasses, his new shoes, etc. He started writing for me without help when I discovered he wanted to be a fireman. He wrote neatly and only asked me for help when spelling hard words.

I was so happy with the change that came over him. His motivation grew. He could write two pages a day by the end of the year. I believe that by using observations, I was able to help him change. Thank you for sharing this technique.

DAWN C. BRAND

I have been utilizing Love and Logic techniques in my classroom for almost a year and it has changed my life. I have not yelled at the students once since I began implementing this program. This has made both the student's lives and mine much better.

A couple of weeks ago our team was preparing to take a field trip to the Natural Bridge Caverns. Since this trip requires the students to be on their best behavior, we developed a system for choosing who would be allowed to go with us. The students were allowed three behavior strikes before they would be out. The students were made aware of this three weeks before the trip.

One boy, who had always had trouble controlling his behavior, had two strikes against him by the third week. In my class, he decided he would throw a pencil across the room to another student. The pencil ended up hitting a young girl by accident and never made it to the student waiting for it at the other end of the room.

I was very calm! I remembered what Mr. Fay had said about delayed consequences and decided this was the perfect opportunity to give it a try.

I called the student over to my desk and calmly asked why he decided to throw the pencil across the room. He replied, "I dunno." I said, "How sad! It looks like that was your third strike and you will not be able to go with us on the field trip." He was very upset by this and began whining about how unfair this was. I replied, "It sounds as though you have many reasons you should be allowed to go, but there has to be a consequence for your actions." The boy looked at me and said, "I know, but I don't want to be the only student not going. Can I have a second chance?" At that point, I told him that this was something that I would have to think about. I would have to get back to him in class tomorrow. Then I said, "It may help me decide what to do if you write and tell me why you did what you did and what you think should be done about it." "All right," the boy said, and then left the classroom.

The next day, he returned to my room at 7:30 in the morning with *three* full written pages about his behavior and what should be done. I showed the letter to my team members to ask their opinion. They were all amazed because this student had never written more than a page in any class all year. All year he struggled with writing, grammar, and spelling and in front of them sat a perfectly edited, three-page paper about this young man's behavior.

By the end of the day, we decided to allow the boy to go on the field trip with us. However, at his request, we called his mother to inform her of his actions and he wrote an apology letter to the girl his flying pencil accidentally hit. Since then, this young boy has improved his classroom behavior and has not sent any more pencils skyrocketing across my room.

I LOVE THIS PROGRAM!
JESSICA GEORGE

Thank you for making such great videos. I'm a fifth-grade teacher, and part of my self-evaluation and improvement plan is watching your videos, which our school bought several years ago. I've been watching one a week, saving it for my Sunday evening entertainment. Much of what you tell me I knew but needed to be reminded of. You've also given me some new ideas.

In addition to thanking you, I want to share a classroom story and problem that you helped me solve. I have a student who is gifted but who has a behavior disorder, and he presents some very challenging teaching opportunities. Lately, he had been belching, spitting, and passing gas to embarrass people or to gross them out. While watching your video, I came up with an approach to possibly solve this problem.

I knew from past experiences that I should not confront the student in front of his peers. I waited until school was out to speak with him, but he, of course, had immediate plans for after school—which turned out to be an advantage, because I called him at home that evening.

The conversation went like this:

ME: Hi, I'd like to talk to you about a school problem. I want to talk to you and not your mother because I want to help your preserve your dignity.

STUDENT: (He's a bit off balance at this point.) Yes? What's the problem?

ME: I've noticed that you haven't been very private with your spitting, passing gas, and belching. I understand that all mammals do these things, including me, but as part of getting along with other human beings, we try to do these things as privately as we can, within reason.

STUDENT: Okay.

ME: I'd like you to think over what I've said, and then write a plan that will help you to do these things more privately.

STUDENT: I can do that.

ME: Would you like to write your plan before dinner or after dinner this evening?

STUDENT: (Pause—he's still a bit confused, but happy to have choices.) After dinner.

ME: Would you like to give me your plan before school starts
           tomorrow or after school starts tomorrow?

STUDENT: After.

ME: Great, and thanks, I can't wait to see you and read your plan. Bye.

I somehow got through the whole conversation without laughing and
with a genuine "lilt" in my voice. He wrote his plan and gave it to me after
the 8:10 bell rang.

My Plan

1. Do it (spitting, belching, passing gas) when nobody is around.
2. If possible, go to the bathroom to take care of these things.
3. Cover my mouth if I belch, cough, or sneeze.
4. If possible, pass gas silently, or say, "Excuse me," in a sincere way.

I am happy to report that for the past week he has been performing his
private functions as privately as possible. He's still probably entertaining
the other boys in the bathroom; however, this isn't a problem and I ignore it.

JIM BABCOCK

As the parent turned and left my classroom, I thought, "Was this little conference for real?" After almost twenty years in the classroom, I believed I
had heard most of the things parents were dissatisfied with concerning
school. But she had a couple of new ones. "Her kid will have it made as a
teenager," I sadly mused. "He will get lots of access to electronic entertainment, won't be checked up on much in school, and will have the
chance to have lots and lots of fun."

During the course of our brief discussion, these were the points she
brought to my attention:

1. "Kids have so much fast-paced entertainment at home. Teachers
   should be able to compete with video and computer games to keep
   the kids' attention."

2. "My kid says that school is boring."
3. "I think teachers should provide kids with more free time for Internet exploration at school. Last year's teacher let the kids play on the Internet all the time."
4. "Kids shouldn't have to do routine stuff at school. They need to spend most of their time having fun."
5. "I'm too busy to come to parent conferences. I just don't have time."
6. "What makes you think you have the right to tell kids to bring cold-weather clothing and boots to school—and to suggest places where they can get such things for less money?"

Of course, we as teachers could only respond effectively to such concerns if we (and the parent) were in the thinking state, rather than the emotional state. I thanked her for taking the time to come in and share her concerns, and couldn't resist slipping in a couple of observations. I kept my words to a minimum, and thought through some other possible responses in my head.

When a parent calls or comes in to express a concern, I first try and find some point on which we can agree. I concurred with the idea that kids had a lot of stimulating, fast-paced entertainment at home, and said enthusiastically, "That's true! We teachers can't possibly compete with what the kids have at home." I indicated that teachers had a responsibility to make school lessons as engaging to students as possible. At the same time, there were parts of school that were necessarily routine—just like the real world. "Most jobs," I told her, "are about 90 percent routine and 10 percent fun—and that's if you're lucky. Many jobs require that the same things be done over and over again. And elementary school is a great training ground for kids. They have a chance to learn how to live with routines. And think about what it takes to keep a home going," I continued. "Meals have to prepared, dishes have to be washed, and clothes have to be folded. I don't particularly find folding clothes to be exciting, but it is a job that has to be done." She really couldn't argue with that and replied reluctantly, "Yes, that's true."

School can provide kids with a great opportunity to improve their skills in task completion and perseverance. Ideally, the school's job is to reinforce these skills that are taught in the home. I find myself suggesting to more parents that chore completion at home has a direct correlation to work completion at school, as Jim says. But more and more children are entering the school system without these skills, and it is an uphill battle for teachers to encourage kids to complete school tasks when kids have had little practice at home. As Jim and Foster point out in *Grandparenting with Love and Logic*, "If respect and responsibility are not the norm at home, worrying about school achievement is putting the cart before the horse" (p. 196).

What about the issue of Internet fun? I discovered that the student in question had never returned his permission slip. So he had, indeed, missed out on the assignments that had involved carefully selected, pre-screened Internet sites. As for free exploration on school time? I don't think so! This might be a great place to use Foster's line, "I see things differently." I'm not the most popular computer teacher in the school when I tell kids that they get to do assignments using sites that I have checked out for appropriate content in advance.

And the winter clothing issue? Oh, it turns out that the student had incorrectly reported that conversation, as he had others in the past. I thanked the parent for coming in to check on things. "It's always a good idea to check out both sides of the story, when things don't seem quite right," I told her. Many classroom situations have taught me that adults almost *never* get the straight story by listening to just one person's point of view!

And the "school is boring" comment? I used to be really threatened by that one. No more. Yes, I need to do all I can to make my classroom an interesting, desirable place for students to be. But even in a classroom with a great climate for learning, a few students are likely to still think that things are "boring." My Love and Logic reply? "Yup! And if you think things are boring now, wait until this afternoon! I'm just getting warmed up!" (Of course, I find other ways to address the "boring" issue with parents.) Some kids find school boring because they do more sitting and thinking about the work than actually doing it. This was certainly the case with the student whose parent came to visit.

I firmly believe that nearly all parents want their children to be happy and successful in school. Sadly, some children do not have the benefit of having parents who show concern for what is going on in the classroom. Some kids may think they truly "have it made" if parents do not take time for conferences, for needed monitoring of student performance, for allowing children to learn about routine work as a part of the real world, and for checking to see if they are really getting the straight story. Our kids may not think so, but they truly *will* have it made when we help prepare them for the real world.

CAROL GWYNN

The first time I ever used Love and Logic principles was during my first summer-school session at a learning center. I had just finished reading the Love and Logic book that my wife loaned me and we had enjoyed listening to several of Jim Fay's tapes while driving back and forth to work. On Friday of the first week of summer school I was shutting down the computer lab when I noticed that several "Intel Inside" stickers had been ripped off the computers and were lying on the floor. At first, although I was upset, I figured that I would have to live with this because I would never be able to "prove" who was responsible for the vandalism. When I got home I told my wife about the incident. I explained to her that it wasn't the damage but the principle that upset me so much. I really wanted to do something, but what? She said, "Well, this would be a good chance to use Love and Logic." So we spent the weekend formulating a plan.

On Monday morning when all of the students were accounted for I got their attention and informed them that *they* had a problem. I told them that someone in the class had chosen to vandalize the lab's computers and I didn't know who it was. I told them that they were free to continue their coursework and that I would register any credits they earned just as soon as the "Intel" stickers were replaced. Finally I said, "If you were not responsible for the vandalism, don't worry. I'm sure the problem will get solved." The students were outraged. It was so unfair to punish the innocent. Blah, blah, blah, on and on. At morning break they were still fuming. However, one of the students came up to me and said, "I tore some of the stickers off, do you know where I might get some new ones?" I told him that I would start by contacting the computer manufacturer. He asked if he could borrow the phone and I told him no because my phone was for official use only, but that there was a pay phone in the hall that he could use. I looked up the number for the company, gave it to him, and he went to make his call.

He soon returned to tell me that he would have to call Intel to get the stickers. He asked me for the number and I told him that it would take me some time to get it, but that I'd try tomorrow if I wasn't too busy. For the next several days, while this one student secretly worked to solve the class's problem, the rest of the class just complained about how unfair I was. In the end the student had to send a letter with the invoice for the computers to Intel to get the stickers. They arrived just before summer school was out and the class was saved. The sad thing is that out of all the students in summer school, only one of them learned a lesson that had "real-life" value.

JIM EVANS

All Love and Logic addicts know the thrill of the moment when an opportunity presents itself to utilize our techniques. The thrill arose for me while serving as the summer-school administrator in a small rural school district in Kansas. The halls were crowded, as usual, with the clutter of classroom furniture and supplies that had been moved out for summer cleaning. The students had been reminded on the first day of classes that these items did not belong to them and they were not to bother anything. However, we had some fifth- and sixth-graders who felt they were exempt from this expectation. The fourth-grade teacher had some brand-new boxes of modeling clay on a table in the hall. As the students left on Thursday, two boys decided they would help themselves. About thirty minutes after the students were dismissed, the teacher came and informed me that some of her clay was missing. (There had been no other students in the building, so the "thieves" were pretty obvious.) I told her not to worry; I would deal with the matter.

I called our local police officer and told him what had happened and what I was going to do. I asked him if he would be available the next morning if he was needed. He assured me he would back me 100 percent; I was on cloud nine! Being fairly confident I knew who the "thieves" were, I arrived early for work the next morning, because I knew these students were always the first to arrive. I took the box that had contained the sticks of clay and sealed it in a clear plastic bag. I had my inkpad opened on the desk and some blank white paper ready to go.

When I saw the first boy arrive, I asked him if he would come into my office to help me solve a problem. He was always eager to help, so he marched in proudly. However, his face quickly whitened as he saw the empty clay box on my desk. He immediately said, "What's this?" I told him that this was what I needed his help with. I explained to him that someone had helped themselves to some brand-new sticks of clay as we were leaving school yesterday. I told him how sad I was that the clay would not be here for everyone to use when the regular school year started in August. I told him I was so concerned about this problem that I had called the police in to take fingerprints from the empty box. I informed him that my stamp pad and the blank paper were there for the officer to use to take everyone's fingerprints. If he found a match we would know who our thieves were. I casually asked him if he knew anything about this. He got so nervous he spilled his guts immediately! This "hardened criminal" told me how he and his brother had taken it so they could share it with others. He told me where every stick of clay was and asked if he could bring it up right after school that day. I told him that would be great and thanked him for his help.

When classes ended that day he ran from the building to his home. He returned in about five minutes with the clay—still in the wrapper. He explained that he felt so guilty about stealing it that he couldn't even have fun with it! This was probably the most important lesson this student learned all summer! Aren't these moments what we all live for?

JOLENE EVANS

I taught a Love and Logic class to some teachers at my school. It is often a "hard sell" to introduce teachers to something new. They feel so burdened as it is, and one more thing can often be too much. So I started the class by talking about what Love and Logic could do for *them*.

Using these principles has made such a difference for me that I want others to know what a benefit it is. My class this year is so difficult that Love and Logic is literally saving my school life. My students have such serious problems that it will take a long time to make a difference with them. But I am already seeing the difference with me.

How Does Love and Logic Help You Take Good Care of Yourself?

1. You focus on what you can control.
2. Children are taught to problem-solve, taking the burden off of you.

3. You upgrade your skills in working with people.
4. You state what you will do, rather than issuing commands.
5. You learn to establish good relationships with students and parents.
6. You learn that you do not have to solve problems immediately. You have time to think, check out options, talk to other people, and reach the best solution.
7. You learn to deal with situations without using anger, lectures, threats, or warnings.
8. You turn more of the thinking over to kids.
9. You eliminate a lot of stress by learning how to defuse arguments.
10. You focus on prevention of problems.
11. You learn the value of questioning to help children come to their own conclusions.
12. You learn how to share information without telling people what to do with it.
13. You learn to show more empathy. As you practice (and even pretend at first), it becomes a part of you.
14. The environment in your classroom dramatically improves. It becomes a happier, more positive place when the anger is gone!
15. Your blood pressure goes down. Your doctor is very happy with you.

CAROL GWYNN

Recently I had a third-grade girl in the office because she had run from a teacher at recess when the teacher asked to visit with her about a pushing incident. When I asked the girl to tell me what had happened, she told me she ran because she did not have to mind teachers that were not her teachers. I told the young lady that at our school, all students were to mind all teachers, even if it was not their teacher. The girl simply refused. I told her the only way she was going to be able to return to school the next day was if she promised to mind all the teachers. The girl told me she wasn't coming back to our school the next day. I smiled and said that would be fine and asked where she was planning to attend school tomorrow. She was unable to give me a response but said she and her mother had talked about her attending a different school. At this point I again smiled at her and said that it would be fine and I just knew she would enjoy her new school, but just in case, she needed to know that she could not return to our school unless she agreed to mind the staff here. Finally the girl agreed to mind our staff members and she was to be allowed to return to our school the next day.

The next part of our discussion was related to how she planned to solve the running-away problem. I reminded her that she could not return to recess the next day if she was unwilling to find a solution to this problem. She simply refused to come up with a solution, so we agreed that she would miss recess each day until she could apologize to the teachers. I completed the referral, smiled at her, and asked which "Thinking Room" she planned to use tomorrow during recess. She told me the room she wanted and I asked her not to worry, that we would have a space available for her tomorrow during recess. She left with the needed paperwork in her hand.

Later that afternoon, just before the dismissal bell, she returned to my office. I smiled and greeted her warmly. She looked up at me and said she didn't need the Thinking Room tomorrow because she had apologized to the teachers and had told them she would be minding them in the future. Again I smiled at her and thanked her for her decision and sent her on her way.

JUDY SPARKMAN, PRINCIPAL

This past summer I was fortunate enough to participate in Jim Fay's fifteenth annual Love and Logic conference in beautiful Copper Mountain, Colorado. I attended with a good friend of mine who is also a teacher. The company and scenery alone were quite refreshing, giving me a wonderful sense of serenity. But the information I gathered there has helped me to gain that sense of being serene and refreshed many times this school year. I teach students with behavior disorders in a self-contained classroom in a public school system, so grasping any kind of serenity throughout the day is quite a feat!

Earlier this year, I had an encounter with a student and at that moment, I remembered a story that Corwin Kronenberg (one of the speakers at the conference) had shared about a young man on a field trip who had knocked down a nest, which caused the eggs inside to break. I remembered how he taught the child to accept responsibility for his actions, rather than punish the student with reprimands and lectures. As I remembered the story I responded in a way much different than what I had ever been taught or had ever experienced myself as a child. The following unfolds the story as best I can remember.

One morning, Johnny had received a fine for an act of physical aggression the previous day. While making his deposit of points, and upon seeing the behavior fine, Johnny became upset. He walked over to the trash can, held his checkbook in the air above it, and looked directly at me as if to say, "Look what I'm going to do!" I was across the room attending another student. Johnny and I made brief eye contact, then I turned my attention back to the student and the task at hand. From the corner of my eye, I saw Johnny drop his checkbook into the trash. I gave him no response, continuing to work with the other student, but I noted in my mind, "Boy, is he going to be surprised tomorrow!"

The next morning when Johnny prepared to deposit his points, he stopped with mouth dropped and eyes wide and stated, "I don't have my checkbook." I replied, "Oh no. What happened to it?" with an emphatic voice as if surprised myself. He simply stated, "I threw it away," to which I empathized, "Oh no, I'm sorry you did that. Now you'll have to start over." He quickly rebutted, "Well, I know how many points I had so I'll just—" but I interrupted him, saying, "Oh, but you can't. The rule is you have to start over. You have no proof of what points you had. You'll need to start a new checkbook." He grew angry, looked at me in a huff, retaliating. I slowly and calmly walked over to his desk and said, "Let's figure out how you're going to get a new checkbook." I then continued, "It takes paper and the copy machine from the school to make a new checkbook. Plus the time it takes for us to make it. We're going to need to figure out how you're going to pay for that." Then I added, "Unless you can think of another way to get a checkbook."

Johnny looked at me, then proceeded in a defiant manner looking about the room as if thinking, "I'm mad! What can I do to show her that?" He focused on something across the room, then charged over to the pencil sharpener and literally tore it off the wall. In response, I again calmly walked over to him, outstretched my arm to escort him, and stated, "Well, now we're going to need to go down to the office," as I guided him through the door toward the office. He loudly attempted to argue with me while walking fast to get ahead of me. He stopped just prior to the office, so I walked around him and over to the door, which opens to a tiny enclosed area used for in-school suspension. I opened the door and looked at him with the confidence that he was going to go in as directed (remembering what Charles Fay had said: "You have to send them the message that you can handle them without even breaking a sweat.").

Johnny did enter the room and plopped into the chair as he shouted, "It's not fair! You didn't tell me!" To which I responded, "I know," and quickly followed that with, "I'm going to give you some time to calm down and to think. I'll be back in just a bit, then we'll talk." Closing the door I told the paraprofessional who had followed us that I would be back in about fifteen minutes, and that if Johnny wanted some paper and a pencil once he was quiet and his three minutes were up, it was okay for him to have them. I told her that when I returned, Johnny and I would talk about how he was going to solve his problem.

When I returned, I entered the room and squatted down to eye level and put a sad look on my face. I paused, then asked him, "Have you figured out a way to get a new checkbook?" He started again with telling me it wasn't fair, that he was going to sue me, and that I should have warned him, to all of which I interjected the one-liners I had learned at the conference: "I know." "How sad." "Bummer." When Johnny paused as if he were done, I softly asked, "So what do you think? What about a checkbook?" He stated with pursed lips and crossed arms, "I'm going to make my own." I answered, "That's a wonderful idea!" At this point I saw that the paraprofessional had brought Johnny some paper and a pencil and he'd begun drawing the lines to make the columns. Johnny then turned his attention back to his paper, asking me what headings went across the top. I asked him if he would like me to get one of our checkbooks to use as a model. He replied, "Sure."

I brought the checkbook model in for Johnny and laid it above the one he was working on. He thanked me, to which I replied that he was welcome. Johnny had started drawing a race car on the construction paper for a cover. I remarked, "Oh, how cool! That's a very nice drawing, Johnny," as I admired it. I then told him that I would be leaving him alone to finish the checkbook. I added, "When I return, we're going to need to talk about how you're going to pay for the pencil sharpener." He was intently drawing but stopped a moment to look at me studiously. "Okay," he replied, and went back to his drawing. We did have that conversation later and decided he would need to involve his parents in solving the problem, they would need to send in the money, and he would have to make arrangements for repaying them. His parents wrote the next day that Johnny would be spending his allowance to pay for the broken pencil sharpener.

Several days later, a few of my students were sharing amongst themselves how many points each had. Johnny calmly made the statement, "I would have had more, but I threw them away." He glanced at me and grinned sheepishly. It warmed my heart to know that he had accepted responsibility for his actions. Several weeks later we had a new student join us. During a class meeting to introduce this child, I asked the students to share some of our rules and procedures. A couple of students volunteered information, then Johnny piped up and said, "And don't throw away your checkbook or you'll lose all your points." As Johnny was talking, he and I made eye contact and he smiled that wonderful smile and I smiled back at him in a way that said, "I'm proud of you!"

I was so thankful for having had the opportunity to go to Copper Mountain and to listen to the Love and Logic speakers. Johnny and I had taught each other a great deal from that one incident. As a teacher in a classroom for students with behavior disorders, I am confident that I will have many more learning opportunities to employ the Love and Logic techniques. It is my goal as an educator to leave every day with the students feeling that they have been heard, accepted, and respected, and treated with dignity.

KATHY A. BILLINGS

I had been watching the Love and Logic tapes for educators and became intrigued by the boy in the school picture and how he solved his problem. I decided to use the example on a second-grader who continually comes to me to tattle (loudly) on what someone else is doing to her. Usually I would have told her to go sit down, or I would have called across the room to the offender to get them to behave. This time I said, "That's too bad. What are you going to do about it?" She gave me the strangest look and actually stopped talking. Then, you guessed it, "I don't know." I asked, "Do you think he'd leave you alone if you hit him? Some kids try that." I used the worst possible solution I could think of, as I'd learned in the tapes.

With a look of disbelief on her face, she quickly replied, "No. If I did that, I'd get despensded!" When I looked perplexed, she said, "That's when you get kicked out of school and they don't let you come back for a few days." *Yes!* She was actually thinking for herself! I continued, "You're probably right, that might not be a good choice. How do you think it would work if you asked him to stop?" Well, she had already tried and that didn't work. I told her to think about it. She went back to her seat but was back at my desk within three minutes telling me what he was now doing.

I started over with the same exact dialogue as before: "What do you think you'll do about it?" "Do you think it would help if you hit him?" I mentioned that there were a few other empty seats she might want to look at, and without a response she was gone. A few minutes later I heard, "Teacher, Cari is in the wrong seat."

It was so great! I couldn't believe how quickly it worked. I had tried ignoring her, asking her to go work it out, asking the offender to keep his hands to himself, etc. None of those things worked, of course. Thanks to these great tapes, I am no longer listening to tattling.

KAYLENE REDD

I just want to write and tell you how much I am enjoying implementing your Love and Logic program both at home and at work. I am employed by the Mesquite I.S.D. in Texas, and it has been my pleasure to spread the "word" about your wonderful program. I have been using your techniques in my own home since the spring of 1997 and what a difference it has made in our home!

One of our campuses, Seabourn Elementary, trained all of their teachers last year using your videotapes for teachers. This campus created new expectations and began to discipline office referrals with Love and Logic. Since that time, I have had the privilege of going to several other campuses and presenting the teacher training tapes and passing out your catalogs with good results.

I want to share a few stories that you might find entertaining. After presenting your tapes to the faculty of one of our elementary campuses, two teachers took the techniques home and shared the following stories with their school counselors.

One teacher has a small baby. Her husband usually doesn't help when it comes to cleaning up after the baby. On this particular evening, the baby threw up in the bathroom and living room. This teacher used implied compliance with her husband by asking, "Honey, which would you rather clean up, the bathroom or the living room?" Her husband looked up from the couch with a rather confused look on his face and after a moment answered, "The bathroom." She was overjoyed. There was no arguing or discussion.

Another teacher was putting her two sons to bed. Both sons were whining to stay up later. The teacher said, "I read bedtime stories to those who are in bed by 9:00 P.M." She did not say another word. She heard the boys saying, "Mom, we're in bed and ready for stories."

Thanks again!
Kelly Smith

I teach sixth grade and had my first Love and Logic class in the spring of 2000. It has entirely changed my method of working with my students. The experience I am about to relate is just one of the many that I have daily now that I am using the Love and Logic technique. One of my students, Dan (not his real name, of course), loves to say "pleeeeeese," which has usually resulted in him getting what he wanted—until now. During a period of morning silent reading, Dan was sitting right by my desk because he will actually read while sitting near me, and at his desk he ends up bothering his neighbors. Our school is about 51 percent free lunch, so the majority of the students eat breakfast at school, including Dan. This is how our conversation went:

DAN: I'm hungry. Can I go to the lunchroom and get a Pop-Tart?

ME: I need you to read.

DAN: But my stomach hurts and I need something to eat.

ME: Did you eat breakfast?

DAN: No, I was too late.

ME: Man, I hate it when I miss breakfast.

DAN: Me, too, so can I go?

ME: I need you to read.

DAN: But I was late and I'm sick. So can I go?

ME: I need you to read.

DAN: But I didn't get breakfast and my stomach hurts. Pleeeeeese?

ME: Don't worry, lunch will be in about three hours.

This type of conversation continued off and on for a good ten minutes. Then he uttered words that I could really capitalize on:

DAN: I'm hungry.

ME: I'm always hungry when I miss breakfast.

DAN: But I was late.

ME: Then you probably had time for breakfast at home.

DAN: Oh man, you always do this to me.

From that instant on, he didn't say another word, but read silently for the remainder of the allotted time. The Love and Logic technique allowed both of us to come out with our dignity, and there were no harsh words, threats, etc., from me.

MARCI BARTU

There were two fifth-grade students that had a physical altercation involving pushing, shoving, and choking just before the end of the school day. The students were brought to me for disciplinary action, as the one thing that will guarantee an office referral is physical altercations. In talking to the two, they were unable to agree on their stories about the events of the altercation. I used Jim's line about "I was not there, so if I believe you (the boy), that means I think you (the girl) are not telling the truth, and if I believe you (the girl), that means I think you (the boy) are not telling the truth." I requested that they spend some time together in the conference room to come up with a written statement they could both agree upon and sign. They were given one pencil and one piece of paper.

Now it was past the end of their school day and I had two sets of parents waiting in the outer office. While the two students reluctantly worked in the conference room, I spent some time with the parents. I advised the parents of the serious actions and requested that they go do errands and return in about half an hour. They agreed and left me with the students. I went in to check on the students' progress and found they were still unable to agree.

At this point the girl asked if they couldn't just pretend to agree, get swats, or something else so they could get this over with faster. I told them I just couldn't leave knowing the situation was unresolved, because there was a strong possibility the same issue would come up again later. I told them not to worry, their parents had all gone to do errands and that I had already planned to stay and work late that afternoon. I left them to their work.

It took about another half an hour, but finally the two returned to my office with a proposed consequence for their behaviors. I thanked them for working out their problem and agreed to their consequence. I never saw these two in the office for an altercation again.

JUDY SPARKMAN, PRINCIPAL

A student in my class enjoys the pleasure of running the lives of his "Helicopter" parents. He is always forgetting something, or whining to them to get his way. One day I had gotten tired of having him call home and have Dad bring something or other. So I began using the one-liner, "You can use the phone if it doesn't make a problem for someone else." I got the reply, "Oh, it's no problem for my dad. He's just home watching TV."

One day we were having this conversation and I asked him how he was going to solve the problem without making a problem for Dad. He said he didn't know, so I asked him if he wanted to hear what some other kids have done. He said yes, so I gave him outlandish solutions, and of course he came up with a much better idea. This happened a couple of times, and then one day our conversation went like this:

FRED: Can I use the phone?

ME: Why?

FRED: I need to have my dad...(do something, I can't remember what)

ME: But that makes a problem for Dad. What else can you do?

FRED: (exasperated) Will you just tell me what some other kids have done?

This boy, when Mom and Dad aren't in his classroom—which they are every Friday—has learned to solve most of his own problems. The Love and Logic techniques are a lifesaver for me in my classroom. When I was first introduced to the techniques at a class last spring, I decided that I would try them out on a very basic situation. I told my class that they could go to recess when they had their coats. I told them I didn't care whether they carried them or wore them. Of course, because that class was full of "keepers," I heard all the excuses. I held firm and told them again that I didn't care if they carried them or wore them. Finally, one of the students said, "Well, do we have to carry them all recess, or can we lay them down?" What a classic question!

MARCI BARTU

I have truly enjoyed using the suggested techniques from Love and Logic. My classroom runs smoothly as a result. I employ the "I noticed" phrase quite a bit and try to reward "good choices" made regularly. The children know it's their choices that lead to the consequences they experience. I rate the program quite highly (on a scale of 1–10, I give it a 9) and plan to continue reading, learning, and using Love and Logic in my classroom.

At the kindergarten level, the children are learning to complete a job at a particular learning center and to be responsible about their time management skills. The children's reward is learning to use their time wisely. A valuable skill they will use all their lives.

I feel I am more successful in reaching my students because I deal with their disruptions calmly and empathetically. I feel bad for them when they make bad choices.

One time when I used empathy on two boys who were going to miss recess due to bad time management on their part (they would have to complete their work at recess and wouldn't get to play), the two boys began to cry. I hugged them, and felt so bad for them, but this made a true impression and they began to use their time more wisely.

The children are learning to make good choices in many ways; as we walk down the hall we are so quiet because I remind them to "make good choices with their voices." Good for them, and good for the children in other classes.

Love and Logic respects the child and forgives the child. Writing a child's name on the board for all to see due to misbehavior is humiliating for that child. I like to send my kindergarten kids home forgiven, and Love and Logic allows me to do that. Assertive discipline did not.

MARINA AMMOURI

My Colorado teaching license was coming up for renewal, and I needed to take some graduate hours to satisfy the state requirements for classroom teachers. I took a class, *Parenting with Love and Logic*. It changed my life. I started reading the materials and listening to cassettes and watching videos. I was afraid to try it, but at the same time champing at the bit to see if it *really* worked. I decided to start on a small, chronic problem in my classroom.

Johnny was one of eight rather nasty children in my classroom. It didn't matter if I was teaching or helping other students; he was always off-task. He also held the honor of being the ringleader of this group. One day I decided to try my new tools gleaned from Love and Logic. We had started our reading groups and naturally, this was the signal for Johnny to start wandering around and getting into trouble. I sat down with the group and started the lesson. After about a minute, I smiled and walked over to Johnny and said in a voice just loud enough for my group to hear, "Johnny, you are welcome to join the group after you have finished your laps." He looked at me and said, "What do you mean, 'after I finish my laps'?" I again repeated the statement, "Johnny, you are welcome to join the group after you have finished your laps." Johnny was so confused, because I was smiling, had a soft voice, and had given him permission to walk around the room.

At the same time, his followers were so confused that they did not get up and join him. They sat in the group and looked at him, waiting to see what he would do. I slowly walked back to the group and asked the second in command to please show me where we were, and continued. Johnny waited another minute and then came over and sat down, mumbling about not doing any laps. That was the beginning of a new relationship with my class.

I used choices, and the four steps to responsibility. Instead of anger and negative statements I used enforceable statements. Changes occurred daily. I kept trying with other children, individually, and then with the entire class. The class worked on problem solving, using the five steps to helping children solve their own problems. I used it with the special needs children. Love and Logic worked like a miracle. My anger was gone. I smiled more, the class laughed more, the children were more respectful. I knew the children were learning more, and having more fun doing it.

I thought, "If this is working well with the class, why not try it with the parents!" Another teacher and I asked the PTA to buy materials for the school and pay for us to attend the facilitators class. In return, we would volunteer to facilitate the parenting class in the evening. Little did we realize what a positive effect this would have on classrooms, our parents, and our school.

Since then, I have facilitated many classes for parents and teachers. I feel blessed to have been able to help so many children, and parents, make not only a positive difference in their lives, but to have less anger, more fun, and enjoy life. Love and Logic did change my life!

ALICE FLOOD

I could hardly believe the words in the popular parenting book I was reading: "Most of the time our kids aren't listening to our words nearly as much as they are watching our posture, gestures, and facial expressions, and hearing the tone of our voice." Albert Mehrabian, author of *Silent Messages,* conducted a series of classic studies and found that the amount of communication actually sent through spoken words is only 7 percent! The greatest portion of our messages—over 55 percent—is communicated through our body language, and 38 percent is communicated through the tone of our voice (Michele Borba, *Parents Do Make a Difference* [Jossey-Bass, 1999], p. 68). This same study was quoted in *Teaching with Love and Logic,* by Jim Fay and David Funk (p. 124).

When I was growing up, my dad would use a strong tone of voice when he wanted to emphasize a point. I remember thinking, "I wonder why Dad is mad?" I thought he was angry a lot, even though I later learned that a stronger voice tone was just his way of making a point. Yes, we learn by modeling, so when I started to teach school, I also added emphasis to things by speaking in a stronger voice tone. Sometimes the second-graders would ask me, "Teacher, why are you mad?" I didn't think I was mad; I didn't feel mad. But the kids interpreted my tone of voice as anger. Our voice tone has a big impact on how children perceive us. I have learned while implementing Love and Logic that the tone of my voice is critical in maintaining an anger-free classroom—both in reality and in the kids' perception. A small laminated card sits on my desk all the time. It fits perfectly on top of the pin box. The card simply says, "Voice Tone." Every time I pass my desk, this little card reminds me that I must watch the tone of my voice, and not sound angry. That "perception becomes reality" phrase comes to mind again.

In addition, how can the Love and Logic suggestion that we "walk up and whisper" help us with our tone of voice? As Jim Fay says, it's impossible to be sarcastic when we whisper. I also think it is much more difficult to have an angry tone of voice when we whisper! Another helpful Love and Logic tip is to teach with a smile. Smiles really help keep the anger out of our voice! Since I started to focus on my voice tone, my class has responded to me much better. And on a few occasions when I have had to raise the intensity of my voice—wow, has it ever had an impact!

Many of the elementary schools in our district are on a year-round calendar, and our preparation days are often scheduled when other teachers' classes are in session. I learn so much from listening to what is going on around me in other classrooms while I am getting lessons ready. (Our school has mostly "open" classrooms.) Listening to others has really helped me focus on my own voice tone. Sometimes we teach with cheerful-sounding voices, and other times we might come across to our students as sounding irritated, angry, or frustrated. If we as teachers have a healthy sense of self, and really want to "upgrade our skills," we might consider having a friend or coworker listen to us over the course of an hour or two (or use a tape recorder), and see what they pick up in our voice tone. We often are totally unaware of how we might sound to kids or other adults.

At the end of each school year, my fifth-grade students talk about the upcoming school year and the teachers they will have. They never discuss a teacher in terms of well-planned lessons, great classroom management, or dynamic personality. They always discuss whether they think a teacher is "nice" or "mean." That perception thing again.

So I will continue to keep the sign on my desk and notice it each time I walk by. My goal will be to have Love and Logic "tools" in my head, empathy in my heart, and a smile in my voice.

CAROL GWYNN

I always look forward to Fridays. Most people don't understand why, because I am a guest (substitute) teacher at a local elementary school. I enjoy using Love and Logic teaching tools. The reason I take delight in my job so much is because Fridays are so unique and diversified with the schedule I am given. I only spend an hour with each class. The teachers switch off and take a one-hour study group each Friday for a reading grant. I get to practice using Love and Logic techniques while guest teaching.

As the weeks go by the children either look forward to the hour with their guest teacher or they dread it. Most of the time when I enter the room the children give me a smile or a little wave. At the end of the day I am always scheduled with Mrs. Horn's second-grade class. They greet me with hugs.

Mrs. Horn's class is known for being a difficult class. It isn't always easy. Like today, for instance. At the beginning of the last hour, I talked to Mrs. Horn before the children entered. I had been thinking, since last week, about a Love and Logic teaching tool I had learned and so badly wanted to implement with this class. I took the time to ask Mrs. Horn if I could experiment with it, and she gave me the go ahead to set things up. She left and I quickly dashed down the hall and spoke with Mr. Sampson. It was all set up; I was ready and was truly hoping that one of the three "big guns," Andy, Sammy, or Josh, would mess up. They would get a chance to learn something while in my tutelage.

Recess was about to end. As I looked over the word-puzzle worksheets Mrs. Horn instructed me to give to the students, suddenly everyone washed into the room like a huge tidal wave after their recess. The yelling and mock fighting were at their normal overbearing level. I was really excited. I knew I was going to get to use what I had planned. Andy was communicating in his usual high-pitched voice across the room to Sammy. Sammy, yelling and laughing, was immediately under his desk clowning around. Drinks, dancing, and darting around were all I could see as I looked across the classroom. Every student ignored me and acted as if I wasn't even there! They thought I didn't know what to do. I guess they thought I was confused. I calmly asked them to take their seats. I was literally talking to myself. I again asked them, with a bit louder voice. Several of these second-graders gave me a casual glance but continued on with drinks, visiting, and loud voices. I tried noticing the students who were attempting to sit quietly. I announced their names, but only a couple more sat down and attempted to listen.

Andy and Sammy had not included the third big gun, Josh, into their clownish antics. I knew I was supposed to choose the most compliant one of the troublemakers to send to recovery, but I am not with this class enough to really know who is the most or least complaint of the three. Finally, I called out Andy's name. He shouted back a rude comment and everyone laughed. I wanted to maintain the good relationship with these boys. I smiled. "Andy," I said, "please come with me." "I'll sit down, *I'll sit down!*" he shouted. He looked around and laughed wildly. I walked toward the door. Andy shrugged and remembered that I had put Josh out in the hall to recover in the past. He decided that he could handle a break in the hall for a bit.

Since I had neither given the children a warning nor threatened them in any way with what would happen if they acted up, I just escorted him out the door. He followed eagerly, looking back over his shoulder, allowing the kids to see his cocky smile one last time. Oh boy did I have to use my self-control! I took a deep breath and cleared my throat. I leaned down and informed him that he wasn't going to stay out in the hall. He smiled and laughed, then all of a sudden, as I invited him to walk with me towards Mr. Sampson's room, his face lost its glow and impish grin. He realized that he was going to another teacher's room for recovery. I explained that he wasn't being punished. He was being allowed time in Mr. Sampson's room to recover from inappropriate classroom behavior. He was welcome to rejoin us when he knew for sure he could use his very best classroom manners for the hour I was to be there. Then came the pleading, "Mrs. Golden, I'm recovered…I promise…look, I really am!" I said, "Okay, Andy, but let's see if you can recover for just five more minutes or so. Mr. Sampson is expecting you. When you can convince him that you can return to our classroom and use your best classroom behavior, you are welcome to return."

When I dropped him off I felt like I was turning him over to the lions. I had explained to Mr. Sampson that he didn't have to scold whomever I sent down, but they needed to have an isolated place to think about how they need to act before they could return. I think Mr. Sampson was having fun with this. He greeted us with a firm face and I turned around and left Andy. I walked a few steps back to my classroom and all of the children were still in their seats. Amazing! They all asked where Andy went. I told them he was recovering in Mr. Sampson's room. At that very moment something happened. It seemed each child turned to stone. You could absolutely hear a pin drop! I looked at Sammy. His darling face was somber. I checked Josh's face quickly and his eyes had that look of concern. Their comrade was sent away. Their leader was gone! What were they to do? Sit quietly apparently, because I didn't hear a peep from them for the next fifteen minutes.

We had story time. In the middle of story time Andy returned, but not without a chat outside our door with Mr. Sampson. Mr. Sampson was really getting into this! As if he had been in the dungeon for three hours, Andy walked in with his face looking very serious. Everyone looked at him. He joined the group and tried very hard to revise his usual behavior. An amazing change took over the entire classroom! The biggest surprise was the behavior of Sammy and Josh. Sammy was absolutely obedient and cooperative. He must have sensed that he would get to learn a lesson with Andy if he hassled me. Josh took his moves from Sammy and it looked like 100 percent cooperation. Their attention to reading earned the class a show-and-tell session, so we went on and enjoyed that.

After show-and-tell we all worked alone and did the word-puzzle worksheet. When the children worked on their own for a short time while, I tested them with some directions. "Children, may I please have your attention? You may work with a partner as long as I see every child included and you use your soft voices. If anyone is excluded we will go back to working by ourselves. It is up to you. Thank you." It worked like a well-oiled machine! They really could follow directions! This was so much fun!

I sat alone doing the worksheet with a mechanical pencil I had found on the floor. Suddenly Andy was by my side. "Teacher…uh…Mrs. Golden, can I work with you?" "That would be my pleasure, Andy." "Uh, Mrs. Golden, that's my pencil you have there." "Oh, I didn't know that, here you go, I'll get another one." "No, that's okay, you can use it." After the worksheet time was over, I handed Andy his pencil and we prepared the room for the end of the day.

When the bell rang to go home, they had their chairs on their desks, their desks lined up, the trash off of the floor, and they were immediately excused. I got a couple of hugs as they flew out the door for the weekend. Andy waited for everyone to leave. He came up to me. "Here, Mrs. Golden, you can have this." He handed me his mechanical pencil as a small gift of friendship. I smiled, "Thank you Andy. I will think of you when I use it."

I walked over to Mr. Sampson's room and told him how well it went. I thanked him. He told me that if I ever needed his help again, just "send them down…"

As I was writing Mrs. Horn a note, she walked in. I told her what had happened and how I handled it. As I told her the events of the hour we laughed and marveled at what the class could really do and how much

Andy had learned. I hadn't had that much fun in that class in a long time. She told me she wished I could teach them all day next Thursday because she was going out of town. I just may call the school and ask them if they have gotten a guest sub for that day. Everyone may think I am crazy, but I just may ask to teach that class the whole day. That would almost be too much fun for a teacher to handle. I think I will take my video camera. Mrs. Horn would have to see their behavior to believe it.

Guest teaching is so much fun when I implement a few simple Love and Logic tools. If I hadn't seen it with my own eyes today, I wouldn't have believed it myself!

ROSIE GOLDEN

I have been teaching kindergarten and first grade in a double-sized, multi-age classroom with fifty children for the past four years. There is another teacher plus two paraprofessionals. However, fifty kids are still fifty kids! Good classroom management is essential for survival in this type of teaching situation. My first year at this school was not the best. My previous Montessori teaching experience did not prepare me for this. I was not very happy and neither were the children.

Between the first and second year at this school I learned about Love and Logic through a college course I was taking. My professor recommended reading *Teaching with Love and Logic* as an alternative assignment. I read the book and knew it was the way for me. Giving children independence and choices, and teaching responsibility, are wonderful ways to manage a large-sized classroom! Letting children solve their own problems gave me time to teach again, which is what I love to do. Some of my favorite techniques have been using statements like, "Don't you hate it when that happens!" for instances of tattling. "I listen to people who have their hands raised," for large group times. And the famous, "Uh oh," when I see children doing something they are not supposed to be doing. We make frequent use of a rest chair for children who aren't ready to be participating in activities; they come back to their work when they feel they are ready. We take a lot of time at the beginning of the year to teach the children to solve smaller problems for themselves. We teach them the strategies they need to be successful.

My second, third, and forth years at the school have been wonderful. That second year, many teachers commented on how much happier I seemed. I was so thrilled with how Love and Logic was working for me that I started to tell anyone and everyone at my school all about it. The third year the school paid for Jim Fay to come and do two in-services, one for parents and one the next day for the teachers. This is an experience I will never forget. I was even able to see Jim in action, as he taught a lesson to a fourth- and fifth-grade classroom.

During my fourth year at the school an awards ceremony was started. One of the honors was the Peace Award. This was an award for a staff worker who best implemented the principles of Love and Logic, taught the children to get along with each other, and promoted peace within the school. I was the winner of the first ever Peace Award at our school. I owe it all to Love and Logic. Without this philosophy I may not have stayed at this school or even in the teaching field at all.

THANK YOU,
SHERRI ROBERTS

Yesterday I did what they call "roving" substitution. Each hour I had a different class, as each of the teachers have an hour's class in this special reading grant the district has received. The first class I had was this high-energy second-grade class. I have taught them before. When I taught them before it truly was a learning experience; however, I was able to enjoy them and I think vice versa (the class gave me a group hug before I left). When I left that day my heart was touched by their hug and tears filled my eyes.

Yesterday I had the same class and when I walked in the teacher seemed glad to see me. When she returned, the children had completed the assignment we had worked on together (I had fun) and she stopped in her tracks when she walked in. I thought at first that something was the matter, so I asked, "Is there something wrong?" She looked around at these quiet children reading in partners... "No, nothing's wrong...but...what is it? What is your secret?" she asked. I smiled. "It's no secret, but do you really want to know what it is?" She replied, "Yes, yes, tell me! The last substitute I had, well, well he just couldn't stand it. He left and never wanted this class again. I mean it was awful…and look at them! They, well, tell me, what is it?" I smiled. "It's Love and Logic. Have you heard of it?" "Why yes, yes I have. I have taken a class, but…" (It's called taking the class but forgetting to use what she learned.)

After our conversation, I quietly went around and bid all the little ones goodbye. As I knelt down to two little girls who had been a bit of a challenge, one said, "Oh no, you can't leave so soon. That hour was too fast…don't leave." My heart ached to stay with them, but I had to go on to the next class. I held her face and told her I loved being with them.

After I got home, I was able to talk to the gentleman who is in charge of doing the two-day training class for "guest" substitute teachers in our district. I told him briefly of the situation of the previous guest teacher, who had not enjoyed himself. I offered my assistance with Love and Logic in the classroom. He was thrilled! He put me on the schedule to speak at the next training session!

Marti Simmons

My sixth-grade class had been working on TAAS "drill and kill" skills, otherwise known as intense review. I sensed the students becoming overloaded and said, "Lets do writing derby for ten minutes." This is a time to communicate through writing only, although the students think of it as time to write and pass notes without consequences. My stipulations are no putdowns and no profanity.

As I was walking the room, I noticed a paper with the words, "Warren," "ass," and "dam." I asked for the paper from the boy and girl, who were partners. They were reluctant but handed it over. This is what it said:

GIRL WROTE: Mrs. Warren gets on my nerves. She get on my brothers nerve too. She always smells like dog pope. She really gets on my dam nerves.

BOY WROTE: Whatever!! You and that dum ass cookie made me sign the stupid behavior book.

I calmly read the script and picked up the cell phone. It was 2:50 and school ends at 3:00. I asked the girl's mom to come into our portable classroom when she picked her daughter up. I also stated that the child was not hurt. "Is she in trouble?" asked the mom. I responded, "I would like to discuss that with you in person but I don't want her to worry about it. I just want her to gather her belongings and sit at her desk until you arrive." I was unable to reach the boy's parents.

When the girl's mother arrived, I gave her the paper. She read it, looked at both students, read it again, and looked at me in disbelief. I stated that I wasn't angry or upset with either student. They knew the rules and chose not to follow them. The consequence was to sign the behavior book (again, because they had disrupted class earlier by talking and sharing a snack during instruction).

The mother said, "I think Mrs. Warren is taking this situation pretty well, considering neither one of you used perfect spelling or word tense. You also put her down although you (daughter) spelled 'poop' as 'pope.' You'll be looking that word up and then writing a paper on what a pope is."

At this time the boy slung his hands and arms with full weight on the desk and yelled, "I sure wish Mrs. Warren was mad or hurt or something. It would make me feel a lot better!"

What could I, the teacher, respond with except, "Probably so." This was a lesson in the benefits of Love and Logic.

NANCY WARREN

Our music class began its symphony unit by playing instrument bingo. Each student had a player's card and a Ziplock bag of beans as markers. At the end of the lesson, I instructed all the students to carefully let all the air out of their baggies and zip them up. Mark'quise carefully blew his full of air and popped it. "That's so sad...I'll just tape it and place it in my grade book," I said.

Next music lesson I said, "Helpers pass out cards and markers...oh, make sure you skip Mark'quise when you pass out markers, he won't need them." Mark'quise asked, "Why don't I get a bag?" "Well, don't you remember? Your bag was busted last class time…but don't worry, I'm sure you will enjoy looking at your player's card and watching the other students play."

After two more lessons of having "fun" watching the others, Mark'quise came to my desk while the game was going on and said, "I forgot to bring a Ziplock bag from home to replace the one I busted." "Mark'quise," I said, "I think that is a great idea!"

Several days later, Mark'quise brought a Ziplock bag to class with his name on it.

ROSEMARY BRUNER

I always believed in setting expectations for my students. Expectations that were reasonable and clear. Expectations that maintained my classroom as a place of learning. Expectations that fostered the growth of positive relationships between my students and myself. Setting such expectations was never a problem. Communication of the expectations to my students left something to be desired. I wanted the communication of these expectations to be memorable, an event, something I could refer back to throughout the year.

However, the idea, the method of communication eluded me. The next school year was closing in. I sat on the couch, wrestling with how I could make teaching my class expectations the event I wanted my students to experience. As I engaged in what seemed fruitless concentration I watched my wife, Shawna, do what she does best. Shawna trains dogs for obedience competition. She was practicing with Cruiser, her 120-pound Rottweiler. Suddenly I had found the experience I wanted for my students. I grinned as I told Shawna that Cruiser would be attending school with me the first day.

Cruiser is not you typical dog. He is enormous, larger than half of my eighth-grade students. Thanks to Shawna, Cruiser is also impeccably trained. I think that he holds more degrees and diplomas than many administrators. Lastly, Cruiser has the soul of a lap dog trapped in his 120-pound frame. These factors make him the perfect candidate for a memorable interaction with middle school students. That was my theory anyway.

After some practice with the dog I put my theory to the test. As I greeted students at my classroom door, Cruiser stood beside me. To say the students noticed his presence would be a vast understatement. Cruiser and I stood in front of the class at the bell. Once I introduced my new teaching assistant and myself the true experiment began.

"Studies have shown that for the most part the intelligence of an eighth-grade student exceeds that of a canine. Believe it or not, you, each and every one of you, are far and away smarter than a dog," I said. The class responded with cheers and laughter at this astounding revelation.

"Since we all seem to be in agreement on that fact," I continued, "what I am about to tell you next should make you all very, very happy. As long as you can all do what Cruiser can do, you will have a fantastic, trouble-free year. Since we have determined that all of you exceed his intelligence level, that shouldn't be a problem."

I positioned Cruiser standing in front of me. "Cruiser, sit please." I asked. Thanks to Shawna's training, Cruiser responded and sat. I looked at the class. "I asked him once. Only once. If I only have to ask Cruiser once to do something, I should only have to ask you once as well."

My wife had also trained Cruiser to respond to hand signals and even looks. I positioned Cruiser standing in front of me again and gave him "the look." Once again, thanks to my wife's training, he sat right away. Again, I looked at the class. "Sometimes I may not ask you to do something. I may just catch your attention and give you 'the look.' This means you need to change something that you are doing. It means I am giving you a chance to fix it with out my special help. If Cruiser can figure out 'the look,' so can you."

Every student in the class was beyond attentive by this point. Every eye focused on the task at hand. Every mind grasping the lesson with clarity. At least that's what I perceived.

Next I asked Cruiser to lie down in front of the class. I placed a treat in front of his nose and asked him to stay. As I walked around the room I asked, "Does Cruiser want the treat?" I got a "yes" from the class. "Why doesn't he eat it if he wants it?" Now the class responded with several great answers:

1. "You told him not to."
2. "He knows he is not supposed to."
3. "He knows you know what is best for him."
4. "He is waiting for your permission."
5. "He thinks he could get in trouble if he does."
6. "He wants to make you happy."
7. "Maybe he knows that if he does what he is supposed to that he might get the treat."

"All of those answers are fantastic. They all could be right. Even though Cruiser really, really wants that treat he won't eat it. So if you see an opportunity to do something you really want to, but you know it's wrong, don't do it. It's your choice. You all have the ability to make the right choice, the choice that will help you succeed. Cruiser can have self-control, so can you."

Now for the grand finale. I gave Cruiser the treat he had been waiting for and placed another one in front of his nose. (This is the part that makes my principal nervous.) I left the students, Cruiser, and the treat behind me and walked out the door. That's right, no teacher. Just a class full of eighth-graders I hardly knew and 120-pounds of Rottweiler.

After about thirty seconds I entered back into the class. Cruiser was waiting patiently for me to tell him he could eat the treat waiting in front of him. My students' jaws were on the floor.

"Sometimes you will be without adult supervision. No one will be here to influence your choices. You probably won't get caught. No detentions, no suspensions. Just you and your choice. You still know what the right thing to do is. Cruiser can manage to behave without my supervision. So can you."

Now I restated the expectations for the class:

1. I only have to ask Cruiser once—I only need to ask you once.
2. Cruiser can understand "the look"—you need to understand what that means.

3. Even if Cruiser really wants something, he waits for my permission—
you need to make sure you have my permission. (I also insert the
students' other comments into this expectation.)
4. Cruiser knows what's right and wrong even when I am not around—
you need to do the right thing even when I am not around.

The students never forgot these expectations. Cruiser became the classroom mascot. Most importantly, the foundation was laid for a fabulous
classroom environment and a solid relationship between myself and each
student in that class.

SAM STECHER

When I first decided to embark on an adventure in the world of substitute
teaching, I was privileged to have had a bit of Love and Logic under my
belt. It has made being a "guest" substitute teacher one of the greatest
experiences in my life.

One day etched within my memory was when I taught a class for only one
hour while the teacher attended a meeting. It was second grade and the
teacher had given me plenty for them to do. This class had several high-
energy students. This day everyone was very cooperative, so I thought.
After the Fit-Kid walk/run, we gathered on the reading rug for a story and
I realized that little Jenny (not her real name) was walking around. I had
allowed all of them to get a drink and settle down after their physical exercise.
I smiled as I invited Jenny to come and sit with the rest of the children.
She did and we started our story. She quickly got up again. I continued
with the story, allowed her to "do her thing," and thought she would eventually get bored and rejoin us at the reading rug. A minute or so later she
started talking and singing. It was disturbing the class and the children
started turning around and laughing. I asked the children on the rug to let
me see all of their beautiful eyes and we would go on with the story. It was
at this time that Jenny upped the volume on the talking and singing. She
added screaming, yelling, and body movements.

By this time, the children on the rug were looking at me wondering just
what I was going to do. I felt my brain thinking, "Love and Logic—Love
and Logic! Choices! Yes, choices!" Knowing that she probably wouldn't

join the class, I gave her two choices that I felt comfortable with. "Jenny, honey, would you like to sit over there in the corner library area and read silently, or read silently at your desk?" No answer. Just more noise and movement. With the loud singing and screaming, Jenny started dancing and moving in just one spot. I was stunned for a second. *Then* she added another dimension to her antics. She laid herself upon two desks that were next to each other and gyrated accompanied by her vocal routine. For a moment I thought she was having a seizure until she stopped, looked at me, grinned, and continued her act.

Again the class looks at me like, "Uh, just what are you going to do?!" I took a deep breath and tried to relax. (Never let them see ya sweat, yeah, right.) I smile. "Jenny, you will be spending some recovery time in the hall. Would you like to walk by yourself or would you like me to carry you?" With that, the noise level continued to rise. If the child doesn't decide which choice is best for them within ten seconds, the teacher does. I moved toward her and she took off like a scared cat.

By now, the rest of the class were on their feet and laughing hysterically. They were enjoying themselves immensely. They loved watching Jenny take me for a wild goose chase, dodging me back and forth and running me around the desks. I couldn't believe I was chasing her! When I realized what I had been sucked into it struck me so funny that I almost joined the rest of the class in a moment of uncontrolled laughter. I stopped and so did Jenny. I slowly walked toward her again and she took off like a flash, only to be snagged by one of her classmates. That little guy didn't know how thankful I was for his generous gift of chivalry! When I reached her she was wiggling and screaming. I gently lifted her (thank goodness she was small). I was able to communicate to one of the kids to bring a chair out into the hall for me. If this didn't work, I was willing to press the call button and ask if she could recover in the office for a while. I wanted to implement the classroom intervention of changing Jenny's location for recovery and experiment with that first.

When we both got out into the hallway, I asked her to be seated. She sat down, but she was breathing hard due to the entertaining aerobic session she had just completed. She looked this way and that. I knelt beside her. I smiled and softly said that I was not angry with her and that she wasn't being punished. I explained that I was just allowing her to recover. I continued to softly ask her if she was ill or if she wanted to tell me anything.

No response. I then suggested that she was welcome to join us when she could control herself and listen to the story with the rest of the class. I gave her one last smile and rejoined the confusion in the classroom.

When I walked back into the classroom the children stopped and were dead silent when they saw me. I invited them to once again sit on the reading rug to finish our story. It was then I realized that I was not going to be able to complete the activities the teacher had left for me to do that hour. I knew she would understand.

A few paragraphs into the story, Jenny softly started tapping from the hall-way outside the door. Then the tapping got faster and louder. Then it crescendoed to a bang-bang on the door. There was that look from the group again. But this time it looked like, *"Oh no! What is she going to do now?!"* I got an idea. I asked the class to help me. I said, "Okay class, this is what I need you to do. I want you to listen to Mrs. Lindquist when I go out and talk to Jenny. When I come back I want you to tell me if I was very, very mean or very, very kind. Okay?" Smile, smile.

They thought this was fun now. I opened the door slowly and there was Miss Jenny looking up at me with her eyes as big as saucers. The entire classroom was quietly listening. I calmly said, "Jenny, honey, would you like to sit here in the hall for your recovery or would you like to recover down at the office?" She just pointed to the chair (she knew I would make her decision for her in ten seconds if she didn't communicate with me— fast learner this kid). I then explained that recovery was a quiet time and that to remain in the hall she needed to be quiet. I once again invited her to come and join us when she could control her actions and have class-room behavior.

I joined the class again and started to ask them how my voice sounded. Before I could do that, all of the children echoed, "You were very, very nice. You had a kind voice." I started to gather the children on the reading rug *again* and then the teacher walked in.

Jenny slipped into the classroom. The little second-graders predictably reported what Jenny had done. All of the children moved about while I explained my concern for Jenny to her teacher. I could see Jenny looking at me and wondering what I was reporting to her teacher. I truly was concerned. The teacher said that the behavior I was describing was totally foreign to

Jenny. I then realized, as I looked upon a now calm little second-grade girl, that it was very difficult for Jenny to have a strange teacher in her classroom. She didn't understand that I was only going to be there for one hour. She had instantly recovered as she watched her teacher enter back into the classroom. The teacher thanked me for handling it the way I did and said that she was going to take precautions and call the parents and make sure that Jenny wasn't facing any unusual family situations. I appreciated the follow-through on the teacher's part.

Later in the day was when I realized how valuable the simple tools of Love and Logic had been. It was lunchtime and little Jenny passed me in the hall. She glanced up at me and gave me a cautious wave. She received a smile and a wink back.

I love teaching little ones. I enjoy using the Love and Logic tools. Together it gives me much satisfaction and gratification. Substitute teaching in our school district is truly one of the greatest part-time jobs I have ever had. How many substitute "guest" teachers can say that and honestly mean it?

MARTI LINDQUIST

In the fall of 2001, I was assigned one of the toughest groups of kids I'd had in quite a while. Two little second-graders were the catalyst. One was a little boy whom they called a "runner." Whenever he became frustrated or angry, he would run out of school, off the grounds and away. Considering I teach in an open classroom without full walls or doors, it was a challenge. I had in my mind he would be my only real problem student when in skipped Kristen, a little redhead with a mission. She pushed the first kid she came in contact with and preceded to put any fear she could into anyone who came close to her. I took a deep breath and wondered why I hadn't taken the disability the doctor had offered me after a bad fall I had had a month before school.

I went through August and September with little doubt I would crash before the end of the year. I tried everything I could to get this little girl to become part of the group instead of always fighting against the group. I could tell she was very angry, but I couldn't seem to get to the root of the problem. One day she got into trouble during lunch and was not allowed to play with the other children. I happened to be in the classroom during lunch (I used that time to lie on the floor to help my back). When she was brought to the room by the recess aide she just stared at me lying there on the floor.

"What are you doing?" she asked. I told her about hurting my back and that I try to do something that helps. As we talked, I asked what things she did when she was hurting. She just hung her head. I also asked what things she thought she would be good at this year. Again, she hung her head. I finally told her I thought she was so pretty and had the most beautiful red hair I had ever seen.

It was then that she picked up her head and yelled, "No, I don't! I hate it! No one in my family has this color hair. I just hate my hair color, you would too if you had it!" As she sat there screaming, her problem became clear. It was like a divine answer I'd been praying for. I looked down at her small, tear-stained face and asked, "What would you think if I dyed my hair your color?"

She looked into my eyes and said, "You have pretty blond hair, you'd never do that!"

"Well, we'll see," I said, and then went on with the day. That night I called the gal who does my hair and asked her to come and take a look at my little redhead. She was able to match the color and I went to school on Monday morning as a redhead.

Some of the boys thought I was a sub and tried some tricks I hadn't seen before. It was a very enlightening experience. As the children realized who I was, they started saying I looked like Kristen's mom. In fact, everyone in the school started saying the same thing. By the end of the day Kristen started acting differently. She wanted to hold my hand when we walked down the hall. She tried her best to get her work done and was even kinder to those around her.

Testing was done on Kristen and she had all the signs of ADHD. I asked if we could wait before putting her on medication and let me try some other things first. (I'm not against medication, except I didn't really believe that it would work in Kristen's case.) I asked her parents to come in and meet with me. They too had been hurt in their educational experience and were ready for a fight. I explained to them that I didn't want to see her on medication. I explained why I had dyed my hair and wanted to see what would happen.

They were so shocked that I would dye my hair for their child that they were willing to do anything. I couldn't have asked for more supportive parents. We set up a schoolwork and behavior chart, which they checked and signed every night. They read with her and made sure that she had her work done. I even let them borrow some of my Love and Logic tapes to listen to. With the growing support she was receiving at home and the acceptance at school, I saw a little girl bloom.

The last day of school, as I was walking out the door to the buses, everyone was shouting with glees of freedom. Then out of the corner of my eye I caught a little redhead huddling in the dark corner behind the door. I slowly knelt down and peeked behind the door and found my Kristen. I asked her why she was crying. I told her summer was waiting and the fun was ready to begin. She once again looked at me with little tears streaming down her face and said, "I don't want to leave school, I love you!" With that she flung her arms around me and hugged me tight. I felt a lump well up in me. I hugged her back and told her I loved her too. I told her we would always be friends and keep in touch. Never had I felt so glad to be a teacher in my life.

I walked to the office where her sister was waiting to walk her home. I hugged them both and waved goodbye. Her mother called at the end of the day too. She wanted to say thank you and return my Love and Logic tapes. She said they had really made a difference at home. I also thanked her for sharing her wonderful daughter with me.

I kept my hair red until school was out. I have spent about $108 trying to get it back to blond (it still has a red tint). Oh well, it's just hair and it will be gray soon enough. Kristen taught me that there are no bad kids, just bad behavior. I know that there is always something that will reach a child; we just have to be listening when it's whispered to us. So, what I thought would be the worst year ever sure had its blessings.

VICTORIA PENLAND

I am a school principal of a K–8 parochial school. We have been studying Love and Logic as part of our regular study group for professional development. During basketball season, our concession stand has deliveries made on Fridays, resulting in cases of soda being left in the gym area. We also run an afterschool care program. One of the afterschool teachers noticed that there was about a half case of pop that was missing. The only people who had been in the area were some of our fifth-grade girls, who were there for basketball practice.

When I received the call, I went to investigate and found that there were several bottles of pop lying on or near the girls' gym bags; other bottles were "stashed" in the girls' bathroom. I knew what had happened, but wasn't sure how to best handle it. I decided to experiment with anticipatory consequences.

I asked the coach to let me speak to the team prior to dismissal. I also asked him not to follow up on anything I might say; to just let me handle the situation. I approached the girls by saying, "Ladies, something has happened, something that is never good. I've noticed that we're missing a lot of pop from our delivery. I'm also noticing that I see a lot of that kind of pop here in the gym. Now, I'm not sure what to make of that, but I'll be spending some time this weekend trying to put it all together. I'll try to decide what I'm going to do about this. But I know you've got a game this weekend, so try not to worry about it. We'll talk on Monday." I then left the gym to a chorus of "What are you going to do?" questions. I only replied with, "Don't worry about, I'll think of something, see you Monday."

My phone rang all weekend. Parents wanted to know what I was going to do. I answered each parent with the same statement. "I'm not sure what I'm going to do. But I know that if the girls come to school Monday with a plan of their own, I'd be willing to listen." The calls intensified on Sunday, parents telling me that their girls were afraid they were going to be expelled. "What are you going to do?!" they kept asking.

I started using the same line on the parents. "I'm still not sure. However, I'll think of something. Tell the girls not to worry about it. But if they want to bring a plan on Monday, I'll listen to it."

Monday came and the girls all reported to the office first thing. Their eyes were all huge and a couple were near tears. "Ladies, what are we going to do about this?" I asked. As Jim says, they gave the only answer they could, "I don't know." I asked if they'd like a few ideas. They said yes. So I gave them a few more questions. "What happened on Friday?" This opened up the flood of confessions. "Sara suggested we take a pop, then everyone else wanted one. But then Samantha got scared, so we hid the pop in the bathroom..." This went on for a while. Then I asked, "What should happen next?" The girls started saying things like, "We should pay for the pop. We should promise never to do it again." The girls were asked, "How would that help solve the problem?" and "Would that be something that you could do?" for each of the options they would come up with.

The girls eventually came up with the following plan: They would write individual letters to the extended-care director, to apologize for doing something that the afterschool kids could be blamed for. They would write a letter to the booster club to apologize for stealing the pop. And each kid would pay for the pop that she had taken. We agreed that we would know the plan was working if the booster club president and the extended-care director both forgave them.

Tuesday morning, I had all the money and the copies of the girls' letters, which had been delivered to the appropriate people. Once it was over, the parents began calling and telling me that the girls had thought of nothing else for those four days. They had called each other to talk about the letters, to decide who had taken how many bottles of pop, etc. In the end, they actually overpaid the booster club, because they wanted to be sure they had paid enough.

This incident won over some of our parents who had been skeptical about using Love and Logic. The "bad guy" became the problem caused by stealing pop. The girls had thought through the resolution, and learned more from this than I ever could have taught them by punishment.

TROY MILLSAP

I teach second grade at an inner-city school on the Hilltop in Tacoma, Washington. McCarver is a school with a student population that is extremely challenging due to the environment in which they live. Drugs, gangs, violence, domestic abuse, etc., are the norm, not the exception.

I have been implementing Love and Logic techniques to working with children from day one of this school year. I have a success story that is virtually unbelievable unless you'd seen it for yourself. Because of the sense of community that has developed among my little darlings in such a short time, I was able to teach an entire day without once using my voice!

I woke up Friday morning with total laryngitis. I literally could not make a sound. I momentarily panicked until I realized that I might have the option of "borrowing" a colleague's student teacher to step in to teach while I directed her. I went ahead and made arrangements for that to happen, but as it turned out, I never needed her at all, thanks to Love and Logic. Instead, I used portable whiteboards and the stationary classroom whiteboard, along with lots of body language, to direct the children in all the tasks and activities for the day.

Those who could read well read each of my written messages out loud for those who had difficulties. Those who were more independent assisted those who needed help with each task. They all gave 150 percent in making the day successful. It was amazing and I truly wouldn't have believed it possible if I hadn't seen it for myself. I give total credit for this miracle to Mr. Fay's Love and Logic techniques.

TERRY ELLEN MCCARTHY

I have been using some of the strategies I learned at the Love and Logic workshop and my classroom seems much calmer. A student who had been suspended from my first-grade classroom for throwing a desk at another student has gone three weeks without any kind of a tantrum. The other students in the class are keeping track and congratulating him every day. When we did New Year's resolutions, one very caring student wrote, "I resolve to help Brandon when he is feeling mad or sad." Just thought I'd share some good news with you.

SHERYL WELLS

PART 5

Love and Logic Works for All Ages

*I*t's never too late to use Love and Logic—it can help our everyday life go much smoother. It can help us avoid unnecessary stress. Sometimes as adults we find ourselves using Love and Logic on other adults. Sometimes, and with great joy, we use it on our spouse. Sometimes we see the influence that Love and Logic has on our grown children. How wonderful to know that by using Love and Logic we have helped a loved one have more joy in their life.

When my husband and I get ready to retire for the evening, we have somewhat of a routine we follow. I work on the computer while he watches his favorite sport of the season on TV. At some moment in time I take him his vitamins, which the doctor suggested he take every night. Without fail it is the same hassle every evening. "What is this?" he asks. "Harry, you know they are your vitamins, you ask me the same question every night." "I don't take those." "Harry, just take the vitamins," I retort while rolling my eyes and taking a deep sigh. "Why?" he asks. "Harry, you have been complaining about lack of energy and this is what the doc suggested, now take your vitamins!" "It doesn't work." "I know, Harry, but pretend they do and please quit this, will ya? I get so tired of trying to do the right thing and you fight me every night. *Now take the stupid vitamins!*" It gets a bit heated, but it has been the same dialogue every night for over a month. I lose it and he wins because I let him get me angry.

Tonight it has got to be different. I have to change, but what can I do? Then it dawned on me! I think to myself, "He is acting like a three-year-old. I am going to try one of my Love and Logic tools...choices... choices...yes, I have to get him thinking." So in an instant I was real excited to experiment with a toddler technique and I couldn't believe the results. Holding the vitamins so he could see them, I said, "Harry, honey, would you like to take your vitamins with cranberry juice or peach drink?" He hesitated a moment and made a face, but this is the answer I received: "I guess peach drink..." I quickly took the cold sweet drink from the refrigerator and poured him a glass.

I walked over to him with a smile and handed him his pills and his drink. Hardly glancing up from the TV he gave me his childish frown. He took the glass of juice in one hand and his vitamins in the other. Again I smiled and he took the pills without a hassle. I could not believe my eyes or ears! I tried it the next night as well and it worked then too. The techniques used in *Becoming a Love and Logic Parent* work whether you are a three-year-old or a grandpa. They just do. And our home is happier because of them.

He got even more stubborn on me after this story was written and I left the situation alone—for a time. Around midnight I awoke him to take his pills. He was *not* a happy camper. My reply: "You are welcome to take your pills before or after you go to sleep. It's up to you." The next night the same thing. I awoke him at midnight. Never *ever* have I had to do that again.

I provide him with a filled Sunday-through-Saturday pill container in his night stand and he takes them every single night without fail. Who says Love and Logic doesn't work?!

MARTI LINDQUIST

Many times when our kids make mistakes they simply did not have all the information they needed to make a better choice. That's why the *Five-Step Problem-Solving Process* is such a wonderful parenting tool. When we get to the part when we ask the child, "And how do you think that will work out?" we often find out that they were lacking important information.

This was clearly brought home to me several years ago when I realized that I didn't have all the facts about tires. My husband and I were running errands together and instead of driving in his car, as we usually did, we drove my van. My husband was driving and we hadn't gone very far when he said, "Chris, how long has your car been driving like this?"

I always hate it when he asks me questions like that because I don't know what the right answer is supposed to be. So I said, "Driving like what?" He said, "Pulling to the side like this..." and he let go of his firm grip on the steering wheel and the car headed off the road. "It must have just started doing that," I replied, but I actually had no idea when it started. It's embarrassing to admit I don't notice things like that.

He saw a gas station on the corner. "I think your right front tire is really low," he said as he pulled up to the air hose. "Oh, I know it's just fine," I replied. "How do you know that?" he asked. "Well," I said, with great deal of assurance, "I just got in the van on that side and if it was flat or low I would have noticed it." My husband sighed. That kind of sigh when I know, deep in his heart he is thinking, "How did you ever get to be a grown-up without knowing these kinds of things." He never says those things, but after thirty-four years of marriage, I can read his mind. So after a pause, he said, "Honey, I keep steel-belted radials on our cars." I replied that I was aware of that.

"Do you understand what that means when there is a steel belt in the tire?" he asked me. "Uh...no," I had to admit. "Well," he began, "it means that you can be driving on a tire that is dangerously low on air, down to even twenty to twenty-five pounds of pressure, but to look at the tire you wouldn't particularly realize that it was low, because the steel belt keeps the tire up. When was the last time you checked the pressure in your tires?" I thought for a moment, and then I remembered: "It was the day we left for St. George, right before Thanksgiving." "Honey!" he exclaimed. "That was nearly five months ago!" "Right," I replied. "And I know for sure that's when I checked them." He quietly sighed again, got the tire gauge out of the lock box, and went around to the front tire.

After a minute, he asked me to get out so he could show me something. I was fairly sure I didn't want to see it, but I got out anyway. "Go ahead and check the tire pressure," he said. I knew this wasn't good, but I checked it, and it only registered seventeen pounds. I knew that couldn't be right, so I checked it again. This time it said sixteen. He filled it with the air hose, and I promised I would go to the tire store the next day and find out what was wrong with it. They found a leak, repaired it, and I was on my way.

Just as it is with so many consequences in our lives, the real learning is often delayed, sometimes for a few days or even a week. In my case however, the real learning was delayed for about four more months. Then the lesson came: on the day my right front tire blew out. I put on the spare and drove to the tire store. I wasn't concerned because I had about 50,000 miles left on a 75,000-mile warranty. The man came out to my van and looked at the tire. "Oh shoot," he said, as he ran his hand around the tire. "There are only a couple of things that will void your warranty, and this is one of them. You see how this tire has worn funny right here? Well the only way that can happen is from driving around on a tire without enough pressure in it. My guess is you were driving around for quite a long while with probably around twenty-five pounds of pressure in your tire." (I didn't want to tell him it was actually seventeen!)

I bought a new tire and learned a couple of great lessons, but the most important one wasn't about the tire. It was about the learning process. Once we have learned something, we assume that any normal, thinking person would know the same thing. But until others have discovered that wisdom or knowledge for themselves, or until someone else has helped them to discover it, people can keep making the same mistake over and over again and never figure out what they're doing wrong. (I have told this story dozens of times in my Love and Logic classes and it is always fun to see how many people in my classes, men included, never knew that information about a steel-belted radial tire.)

When we walk kids through the problem-solving process, it will often illuminate the problem in their thinking process and open up a whole new way of doing things.

CHRIS HALL

I fully expected to leave Love and Logic behind when I went on vacation. The school year ended, I put my books and papers aside, and packed for the adventure of a lifetime—a trip to Alaska. But as it turned out, some Love and Logic slid into my roller bag, alongside my wool socks and hiking boots.

A couple of days into our wildlife-watching trip, we went to eat at a nice seafood restaurant. One of the tour leaders had a lot to drink at dinner, and as we were ready to leave, he hopped into the driver's seat of the van. Big problem for me. I thought back to what I had learned about "I messages" and decided to try one. The other option was a very expensive cab fare back to the hotel. As the driver was about ready to start up the van, I said to him quietly, "I am not comfortable riding with drivers who have been drinking alcohol. Would you change drivers?" He looked back at me and said, "Oh, sure. No problem." The nondrinking driver took over, and we went on our way.

Later in the tour, I was assigned a roommate who had a very challenging, hard-to-please personality. As we arrived at the cabin where we were going to stay, I decided to give her as many choices as I could think of for getting settled in the cabin, and she was happy with that. Then I set up shop in the other corner. When her nonstop talking started to drive me nuts, I kept thinking, "You cannot control what she does. But you can control *your* location!" So I would quietly excuse myself and go walking for a while. Then my brain could rest, and the voracious Alaska mosquitoes could have an extra feast.

On another occasion, there was some disagreement on a proposed change in the itinerary. An opportunity had come up to see a much-wanted bird in the area, and the leader didn't want to take us there. I was able to put Foster Cline's excellent phrase, "I see things differently," to use. It did not change the outcome, but I could state my case without becoming angry. At the end of the tour, I needed to store my luggage for a few hours before flying home. It's amazing what a positive response you can get from a harried desk clerk when you start your request with a very polite, "Would you be willing to...?" and then finish with, "Thank you very much. I really appreciate your help."

The scenery was unmatched, the wildlife was exciting, and Love and Logic helped smooth over the challenges of spending two and a half weeks traveling with an eclectic group of folks!

CAROL GWYNN

I have just finished reading the current issue of the *Love and Logic Journal*. As usual, it was enjoyable as well as helpful. About ten years ago, the "word" came down that foster parents would no longer be allowed to use spanking as a means of discipline. Although we were using other methods besides spanking, we were reluctant to give it up completely. Our first reaction to the news was, "Well, we will just quit fostering." However, after giving it some thought, we decided to find other methods of discipline. Our family enjoyed fostering, felt we did a good job, and also found it rewarding in many ways.

The search began. First we attended a seminar on Dr. Cline's book *High-Risk Children Without a Conscience.* I found so many of my children in his book. While at the seminar we purchased Jim Fay's audiocassette *Helicopters, Drill Sergeants, and Consultants.* We were hooked on this new method of Love and Logic.

You ask how Love and Logic has changed our lives? We have used it many times. Most recently, our four-year-old foster son decided he could not dress himself. I set the timer and told him we were leaving when the timer went off, dressed or not. Having to finish dressing in the car with a seatbelt on was not easy. He dresses himself each morning with "no problem" now. How has Love and Logic changed our lives? Well, we are still fostering.

This is our thirty-second year. Our longevity is partially due to your Love and Logic ideas. Thank you!

SINCERELY,
FRED AND BARBARA FREEMAN

The "tell them what you'll do" worked on my husband. Our children are all grown, so I practice the techniques on him, *and they work!* My dear husband developed a habit of putting his dirty clothes on the floor across the six-foot hall from the dirty clothes hamper. One day I said, "I'm going to wash all the clothes that are in the hamper." I really didn't think another thing about it, but when I came upstairs to get the clothes, all his were picked up and in the hamper. What a sanity-saver this technique is. I could go on and on. Thanks again for a wonderful new way of dealing with problems.

MARCI BARTU

I have just received the most wonderful gift. I got off the phone with my adult daughter Mali (pronounced "Molly"), age twenty-three, a few minutes ago. We visit each week on the phone and tonight she made me smile.

She was telling me about what happened at her work. Her job is telephone customer service with a credit card company. This is how the conversation went:

MALI: Oh, Mama, when I hung up from helping a lady customer the other day, I just said right out loud, "I love my mom."

ME: Really? That is so sweet, Mali. What made you say that?

MALI: Well, this lady I was helping was being *very* rude to me. She talked so impolitely and I just said to her, "I will be more than happy to help you take care of your problem when your voice is as respectful as mine. It is up to you." And Mama, you know what?

ME: What, sweetheart?

MALI: She said, "Oh, I'm sorry, I apologize," and I told her "thank you" and we went on to take care of her situation and I never had another problem with her. When I hung up after helping her I just had to say out loud that I loved my mom because I had heard you say that so many times in our home and it just came so natural to me.

The gift of hearing my adult child reflect back to her teenage years when I, her mom, was using the Love and Logic basic principle of taking good care of myself, is a moment to behold! How wonderful to hear her taking good care of herself as an adult in this big world. This conversation gave me the opportunity of expressing my deep gratitude to her for being my daughter. I told her how happy I was that she is now able to take good care of herself and be an example to her son.

This way of "being" does not stop with our behavior toward others. It continues on. I didn't know when I would see the fruits of Love and Logic in my children's parenting abilities. Tonight I know that my grandson will learn how to take care of himself as he watches his mother's example.

After I was told this lovely story by my daughter, I hung up the phone and realized that when I took care of myself, I taught my children to take care of themselves also.

With a few more kind words and sweet voices…this world can and will be a better place.

MARTI LINDQUIST

One night as I was leaving the room, I noticed two women sitting at a table in the back. One of them was trying to comfort the other, who was crying and was obviously very upset. As I passed by the table they looked up at me and I said, "Bad day?" The upset woman began to tell me of a very difficult experience that had happened that day with her daughter. Both of the women were personal friends of mine, so I sat down for a few minutes so that we could visit about it. Time got away from us and before I realized it, it was past 10:00 P.M. The custodian appeared in the doorway. I felt a little embarrassed that we had kept him in the building for so long. I looked up and said, "I'm sorry we're so late getting out. Would you like us to all go home now?"

He looked at us kindly and said, "No, no you're fine. I just needed to let you know that I have already set the alarm, so if you're still in the building in five minutes, you will need to sit very still until tomorrow morning at 6:00 A.M."

As we hurried out the door, all laughing, and quite impressed with his delightful way of getting rid of us, my friend realized maybe that was all she needed to do with her daughter: find ways to set limits that really were enforceable.

CHRIS HALL

Doesn't it seem like some of life's biggest challenges come as we try to get along with other people? Interactions between parents and children, teachers and students, bosses, employees, coworkers, people at church, the folks at the grocery store—the opportunities for positive (or negative) interactions are almost endless.

Can our Love and Logic skills help us improve our interactions as adults? I would give a resounding "Yes!" to that question. Love and Logic could be as beneficial as taking a social skills class.

First, Love and Logic teaches us to interact with others without anger. Maybe we should take one of those leftover computer labels and type, "No anger, lectures, threats, or warnings..." and put it on the dash of our car. Learning to get our adult problems solved without anger—what a valuable skill to have! We can return the defective item to the store without blasting the clerk. With practice and effort, we might even be able to smile when someone cuts us off on the highway. And the ultimate test—can we make it through the lines at the Department of Motor Vehicles without anger? That feat might be enough to give someone an automatic pass through the pearly gates.

A while back I was listening to Foster Cline's audiocassette *Lying, Cheating, and Stealing*. No, it wasn't me doing the stealing; it was a pair of students in my classroom. From this tape, I picked up a jewel of a phrase that I have used several times since: "I see things differently." These words have served me well in a couple of situations that could have become confrontational. There will be situations where we will *never* see eye-to-eye with another person. A corollary to this phrase that works well for teachers when dealing with parents is, "This is what I observe in the school setting. You may or may not be seeing this behavior at home." That allows you to state your case without the other person becoming so defensive.

How do you think adults view the issues of control and choices? I saw a powerful example of this at church. Our congregation has traditionally had two or three adult Sunday School classes, and people could attend whichever one they wished—or they could switch back and forth. On a particular Sunday, people came to Sunday School—and there was only one class offered. Many people were unhappy. Even mature, responsible, thinking adults like to have choices. I believe that many adults are as responsive to Sylvia Rimm's "Control V" as children are; they do not like to have their freedoms, once granted, taken away.

What about the issue of control in adult relationships? Books can be (and have been) written on this topic. How many relationships have been totally shattered over the issue of control? How many people have to "win" at all costs? How much better off we would all be if we could learn to give away some control, as Love and Logic advises. Many people in families with highly controlling spouses or parents feel that their opinions are not valued. This can have lifelong implications for a person's self-esteem.

I've seen some situations where giving away control literally changed the outcome for the better. While conducting parent conferences, I found that starting the conference with this statement made things go much better: "I want to make sure that your questions and concerns are addressed first." I would then turn the conference over to the parent. Nearly every time, the parent would bring up the same concerns that I had as a teacher. And the parent would feel that he or she was being listened to. Another example: I take music lessons from an outstanding teacher. Not only is she a highly proficient professional musician, but she also allows her students (nearly all of us are adults) a great deal of latitude in the music that we choose to learn. She makes suggestions, but we get to decide what we want to play. And it stands to reason that a person will practice harder on a piece he or she really enjoys and wants to learn!

What about the politeness and consideration for others that Love and Logic teaches? I don't think that adults like being ordered around any more than kids do. If we incorporated such phrases as "Would you consider...?" "What would be best for you...?" "How would this work out for you...?" into our interactions with spouses, bosses, coworkers, and others, we would most likely get more cooperation. And we can't forget the power in using lots of questions, rather than just giving orders.

I have seen the use of empathy work miracles with upset adults. One evening, a customer came into the grocery store where I work part-time. She was livid; she said that her dinner party had been ruined by the food she purchased at our store. She slammed a package of shrimp down on the counter, and angrily demanded restitution for the shrimp. My first words were, "I'd be really upset, too, if that happened to me. That is terrible to have a party ruined after you've gone to all that work. I know that it is too late for the party, but would you like replacement food items, or a refund?" She calmed right down, and was able to respond in a civil manner. When people are upset, it often works to *agree* with them. Then, when they are out of the emotional state and into the thinking state, we can actually work on solving the problem.

It is hard to rank the valuable techniques that Love and Logic teaches, but I think "controls versus wishes" is one of the best. This one has the potential to save a lot of rocky marriages. "What can I control?" "What do I wish I could control?" The bottom line is—we can really only control ourselves. In troubled relationships of all kinds, we are the ones who have to make the decision to change. Often, our positive changes lead to changes in the other person. And we simply have to let go of many things that we cannot control or change.

I initially was introduced to Love and Logic as a set of practical ideas for working with children at home and in the classroom. In the years since that time, I have used Love and Logic effectively in many other situations involving adults—with excellent results. An old cereal ad said that this particular brand "isn't just for kids." And Love and Logic isn't just for kids, either.

CAROL GWYNN

161

Index

Each year parents and educators across the country attend *Becoming a Love and Logic Parent* classes. For information on classes or to find a facilitator in your area, phone the Love and Logic Institute at 800-338-4065.

Love and Logic Seminars

Jim Fay and Charles Fay, Ph.D., present Love and Logic seminars and personal appearances for both parents and educators in many cities each year.

For more information, phone the Love and Logic Institute at 800-338-4065 or visit www.loveandlogic.com.